Front cover:
The Tiger (released 11 September 1913).
Vitagraph one-reeler. This scene was shot
with a combination of diffused fill light and
directional highlights. (Page 431)

This issue:
International Cinema of the 1910s

Edited by Kristin Thompson

Editorial office:

Richard Koszarski
Box TEN
Teaneck, New Jersey, 07666, USA
E-mail: filmhist@aol.com

Publishing office:

John Libbey & Company Pty Ltd
Level 10, 15–17 Young Street
Sydney, NSW 2000
Australia
Telephone: +61 (0)2 9251 4099
Fax: +61 (0)2 9251 4428
E-mail: jlsydney@mpx.com.au

Other offices:

John Libbey & Company Ltd
13 Smiths Yard, Summerley Street
London SW18 4HR, UK
Telephone: +44 (0)181-947 2777
Fax: +44 (0)1-947 2664

John Libbey Eurotext Ltd, Montrouge, France
John Libbey - CIC s.r.l., Rome, Italy

Printed in Australia by
Gillingham Printers Pty Ltd, South Australia

An International Journal
Volume 9, Number 4, 1997

This issue:
INTERNATIONAL CINEMA OF THE 1910S

THE UTS REVIEW

Cultural Studies and New Writing

Edited by Meaghan Morris and Stephen Muecke

The UTS Review (University of Technology, Sydney) is a new and important Australian journal, the emphasis of which is on works that engage with contemporary issues. The journal is a 'review' in the fullest sense. We encourage serious discussion of new publications in cultural studies as well as of books or cultural events of public interest and we prefer reviews written in a spirit of care and responsibility, not malice or anxious self-censorship. We also seek reviews and translations of work.

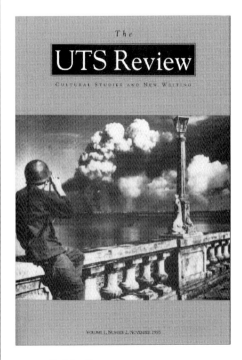

Writers working in English face the problem of being published as there are fewer places in which to publish than there were ten years ago. It is difficult enough for established writers to publish serious works, but even more difficult for young academics and new writers. *The UTS Review* offers an international space for academic and creative writing on culture to receive critical discussion.

The UTS Review has a regional rather than nationalist outlook, with interest in writing that shapes new relationships betwen social groups, cultural practices and forms of knowledge. It is a journal which will be of interest to librarians and to academics and students in Aboriginal Studies, Anthropology, Archaeology, Arts, Humanities, Language, Literature, Communication and Human Science, Cultural Studies, Education, Multicultural Studies, Media and Communication Studies along with Sociology.

Available from:
John Libbey & Company Pty Ltd, Level 10, 15–17 Young Street, Sydney NSW 2000 Australia.
Ph: +61 (0)2 9251 4099   Fax: +61 (0)2 9251 4428   E-mail: jlsydney@mpx.com.au

ISSN 1323 1677

Subscription rates in Australian dollars (includes postage)
Individual AUD$37.00   Institutional AUD$50.00   Back issues AUD$19.00

Subscriptions in US dollars, Europe & North America (includes surface postage)
Individual US$37.00   Institutional US$50.00   Back issues US$19.00

Rest of the world (includes surface postage)
Individual AUD$47.00   Institutional AUD$64.00   Back issues US$19.00

For airmail, please add AUD$20.00 per subscription (N. America US$15.00).

Film History, Volume 9, pp. 339–340, 1997. Copyright © John Libbey & Company
ISSN: 0892-2160. Printed in Australia

International cinema of the 1910s

n a sense, the 1910s were the last decade of film history to be rediscovered by scholars. For years, that decade's importance lay primarily in a few classics – *Cabiria*, *The Birth of a Nation*, *Intolerance*, *The Outlaw and His Wife*, and the short films of Charlie Chaplin. Many of the rest of the films were the stuff of legend, still lying in archives untransfered to preservation copies. Mary Pickford even locked away all the films whose production she had controlled. The 16 mm collectors' market was one of the few ways to see films from the era, but these prints were often tattered and/or corrupt versions.

A growing openness in film archival policy and a wider support for preservation and restoration has helped to change this situation dramatically. And, a series of retrospectives held by the silent-film festival, 'Le Giornate del Cinema Muto' in Pordenone, Italy, has provided a major way of bringing these newly available films to wide attention. What the 1978 FIAF conference in Brighton did to bolster interest in the earliest cinema, the Giornate programs have done for the 1910s.

Though often including films from early periods as well, Pordenone's big national retrospectives tended to include more films from the 1910s. Each provided an overall sense of one nation's production, but also revealed at least one major new filmmaker: Georg af Klercker in the 1987 Scandinavian season, Evgeni Bauer in the pre-Revolutionary Russian program (1989), and Franz Hofer in the pre-*Caligari* German retrospective (1990). The 1910s Hollywood season (1988) and the De Mille program (1991) combined to reveal the enormous variety and sophistication that the American cinema had reached at a remarkably early date. Suddenly Griffith's great mid-decade features had to be seen in a whole new light. Indeed,

it seems appropriate that Le Giornate should now launch out toward the goal of showing all the extant Griffith films (beginning at the 1997 festival, still upcoming as I write this).

Naturally the revelations at Pordenone and from elsewhere inspired expanded research in this period. Although each Giornate festival was accompanied by extensive publications, much remains to be done, and indeed the intervening years have seen considerably more attention paid to the 1910s. This issue of *Film History* was intended to provide an outlet for some of this work.

With a lot (though certainly not all) of the more generalised spadework done, one might expect to see more small-scale, in-depth studies of individual films and specific subjects. Indeed, the essays published here all demonstrate that this is the case.

David Williams re-examines the significance of the *Cinematograph Act* of 1909 (the consequences of which occurred in the 1910s) and offers a new interpretation of its effects; he argues that in addition to allowing local control of safety measures, it also had the unintended result of allowing more local control over programming. Shelley Stamp Lindsey also deals with the struggle for control over exhibition, in this case by offering new material and insights on the reception of and controversy over *Traffic in Souls* in New York City.

One phenomenon that occurred in a number of countries during the 1910s was a new debate over claims that that movies could be developed into high art. This trend included discussions of the *Autorenfilm* in Germany in 1913 and theoretical articles by Louis Delluc and other French writers and filmmakers later in the decade. Joanne Bernardi examines a similar phenomenon in Japan, the debate over the concept of the 'pure film' in Japan during the 1910s; she also adds a primary resource to the small body of work available for the study of this period, with a translation of a script for Norimasa Kaeriyama's lost 'pure film', *The Glory of Life*.

Ben Brewster continues his work on the early feature film with an analysis of Maurice Tourneur's *Alias Jimmy Valentine*. He deals with the relationship of nineteenth- and early twentieth-century theatre to early features, focusing on 'situational dramaturgy', an approach to narrative that he developed with Lea Jacobs.

My own essay examines how narration works in three Vitagraph films from 1911, 1912 and 1913, seeking to show how techniques for presenting story information changed rapidly during an era when filmmakers were exploring what were to become the guidelines of classical filmmaking.

This issue of *Film History* will, I hope, be only one of many publications that continue to clarify the 1910s. Even as it goes to press, the rediscovery continues as a substantial program of Mary Pickford's films commences a tour to American archives, museums and universities.◻

Kristin Thompson

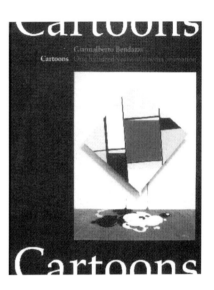

Film History, Volume 9, pp. 341–350, 1997. Copyright © John Libbey & Company
ISSN: 0892-2160. Printed in Australia

The Cinematograph Act of 1909: An introduction to the impetus behind the legislation and some early effects

David R. Williams

t is a widely held assumption that the *Cinematograph Act* of 1909, in the United Kingdom, was the watershed between the 'penny gaff' and the established cinema, between the showman and the manager. It is the purpose of this brief article to demonstrate that, while the intention of the Act could be seen as a national tidying up of existing professional practices, local by-laws and local regulations for the safety of the public, its unintentional result was the controlling powers it gave to local authorities to determine programming as well. The Act itself enabled the Secretary of State for Home Affairs to make regulations concerning the safety of buildings, projection room enclosures and the operational processes when cinematograph performances using inflammable film were taking place. Each building or structure would need to have a certificate of compliance which could be submitted to a local controlling body delegated to issue Cinematograph Licences.

Cinematograph performances had a perceived history of being potentially dangerous. International reporting of the Charity Bazaar Fire in Paris on 4 May 1897 had alerted the public to this danger. Graphic artists' impressions of the confla-

gration that killed perhaps 140 people (not only in the cinematograph booth but in adjacent stalls, too) became almost symbolic icons of the hazards of cinematograph performances.

Cinematograph film was highly inflammable when exposed to heat. George Henderson, a turn of the century cinematograph showman in Stockton-on-Tees, County Durham, used to astound his audiences by spectacularly putting a match to a strip of film which he held in his gloved hand. If cinematograph film jammed in the projection gate and was not swiftly released, combustion from the heat of the lantern house could take place within four or five seconds. The normally employed limelight illuminants were unpredictable in confined spaces. A

David R. Williams is the retired Head of The Film and Television Department of the College of St. Hild and St. Bede, Durham University. In the 1950s, he was a founder member of the now defunct Society for Film History Research. He is currently researching the history of cinema exhibition in Durham City with particular reference to the attitude of the Church to this new form of entertainment. Correspondence to 17, Wearside Drive, Durham DH1 1LE, UK

Fig. 1. The burning of the Theatre Royal, Exeter, September 1887. From *The Ilustrated London News*, 10 September 1887.

lighted gas jet projected onto a lump of lime held in a clamp produced an intense white light. Though the commonest illuminants were controlled mixtures of acetylene and oxygen, or oxygen and hydrogen, other more volatile gases such as ether could be employed. Theatrical fires often caused by exploding limelight fixtures were commonly reported long before the invention of the cinematograph. The destruction of the Theatre Royal, Exeter was sufficiently alarming to be featured in *The Illustrated London News* of 10 September 1887.

The Newmarket Town Hall cinematograph fire in September 1907 was widely reported across the whole of Britain and was sufficient to revive press and public fears about the safety of film shows. Hannah Starling was the only fatality, but alarmist newspaper reports gave the numbers of injured as greater than that of the actual audience. *The Kinematograph and Lantern Weekly* provided the industry's view, that the accident was not truly attributable to the cinematograph itself.[2] At the interval, the audience began to move towards the single exit behind the projector before the house lights had been fully raised. Someone pushed against the cinematograph, and the rubber tube connecting the hydrogen gas cylinder to the lamp house jet was

pulled off. The gas ignited and set fire to the film. The sudden flame panicked the audience, and though the film was quickly extinguished several people were burned, and others injured in the rush to escape. The showman, Mr Court, had, in fact, got a portable operator's box but the size of the hall, he had said, made its use impossible. Evidence at the inquest confirmed that it was the call of 'Fire' and the resulting panic that precipitated the tragedy, though the technical evidence pointed more to a piece of white-hot lime falling from the lantern.

Further comment in *The Kinematograph Weekly* of 19 September 1907 did not belittle the fire risk and suggested that the invention of non-inflammable film would do away with the hazard. In the same issue, the editor commented that the London County Council (LCC) regulations for public safety on licensed premises had proved effectual. Had these been in force at Newmarket, the accident could not have happened. However, he warned against the enforcement of regulations that would 'hamper the profession'.

The LCC regulations dated from December 1898, October 1900 and January 1906. No cinematograph performances could take place 'involving the use of a lengthy combustible film' on premises licensed by the Council unless 'all reasonable precautions had been taken against accident and danger to the public'. Notice of at least three days was to be given to the Clerk of the Council before an exhibition was to take place, and the Council's inspector had to be afforded access to inspect the apparatus. The apparatus had to stand in a suitable fireproof room or inside an operator's box which had sufficient room for him to operate freely. The box had to be fireproofed and the self-closing doors had to open outwards. Three windows were required at the front of the box not more than eight inches square, (205 mm) and windows at each side were not to be more than six inches square (150 mm). They needed to have safety flaps that were closeable from the inside and from the outside. Other parts of the regulations referred to safety apparatus on the projector and the use of take-up spools; the storage and rewinding of spools in a place separate from the box, the employment of a minimum of two operators and the enforcement of a no-smoking rule inside the box. The regulations recommended the use of electric arc lights for the illumination of the lantern. Ether or inflammable liquids were prohibited as lighting sources. As an alternative light source, British Oxygen were selling a gas jet that they claimed could produce from 1800 to 2000 candle power using town gas and an oxygen cylinder. Arc lamps using direct current electricity from on-site generators or direct from the mains were also in use.[3]

In an article by a barrister in *The Kinematograph and Lantern Weekly* in November 1908, the extent of the licensing regulations was summarised.[4] The LCC regulations could be enforced under the *Disorderly Houses Act* of George II or by a number of public health Acts. The entertainment essentially must contain 'dancing, singing, music or other entertainment of a like kind'. The problem was that there was not sufficient case law to decide whether a piano accompanying a film was an essential part of the entertainment or a subsidiary to the performance. The law did not apply where the use of the room was merely occasional or temporary. There was no firm opinion as to whether once a week or once a month could be considered habitual.

The introduction of non-flammable film and a new device for the 'automatic extinguishing of fires in cinematographs' appeared to offer salvation. The device was demonstrated in December 1908 at the Hippodrome, London. It appears to have produced more dissension than enlightenment, since, according to the *Kinematograph Weekly* report,[5] there were so many experts there that they soon split into little disputing groups. The device itself was a receptacle filled with water and suspended above the cinematograph much like a flushing cistern. Beneath it was a sprinkler that was activated by a cotton cord. When flames burned through it, the sprinkler valve opened and drenched the apparatus, thus putting out the fire. Many of its critics declared that there were other ways of putting out the flames than drenching a valuable piece of equipment in water and destroying perhaps £50-worth of film. A comparative demonstration of other devices was promised for a meeting in the next week.

As a result of the demonstration, Mr Walter Reynolds, the LCC expert on these matters, added three new regulations to those already existing:

1. All machines must be fitted with two metal film boxes with narrow film slots and closing doors to prevent fire passing into the boxes.
2. All films not on the machine must be stored in metal boxes.
3. The film gate shall be sufficiently narrow to prevent flames travelling upward or downward.[6]

In an interview given to the 21 January issue of *The Bioscope*, Walter Reynolds, sometimes referred to as the Father of the *1909 Cinematograph Act*, outlined his case for legislation. He observed that there were hundreds of unlicensed premises in London showing films without adequate protection for the public. It was ridiculous that the only licensing Act on which councils could take action was the *Disorderly Houses Act* of 1751. Twentieth-century amusements needed twentieth-century regulations. Even then the regulations were outdated. If a pianist was employed, a licence would be needed, but not if a mechanical piano was providing the music. In some areas, simply putting up a notice which said, 'No Dancing Allowed', deregulated the hall. Walter Reynolds urged exhibitors to give support to a campaign which would rid the industry of the undesirable operators who brought it into disrepute.

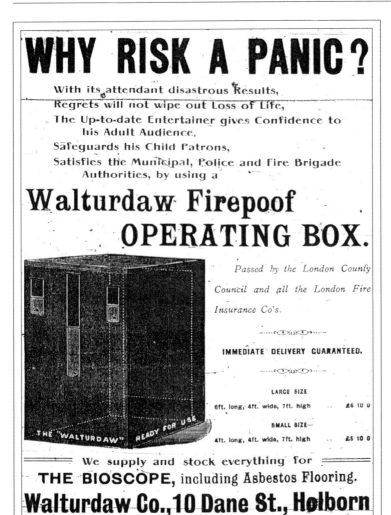

WHY RISK A PANIC?

With its attendant disastrous Results,

Regrets will not wipe out Loss of Life,

The Up-to-date Entertainer gives Confidence to his Adult Audience,

Safeguards his Child Patrons,

Satisfies the Municipal, Police and Fire Brigade Authorities, by using a

Walturdaw Firepoof OPERATING BOX.

Passed by the London County Council and all the London Fire Insurance Co's.

IMMEDIATE DELIVERY GUARANTEED.

LARGE SIZE

8ft. long, 4ft. wide, 7ft. high .. £6 10 0

SMALL SIZE—

4ft. long, 4ft. wide, 7ft. high .. £5 10 0

We supply and stock everything for **THE BIOSCOPE, including Asbestos Flooring.**

Walturdaw Co., 10 Dane St., Holborn

Telegrams: ALBERTYPE.   Telephone: 4707 HOLBORN.

Fig. 2. Advertisement for the Walturdaw Fireproof Operating Box. From *The Bioscope*, 18 September 1908.

seven days' notice.[7] The Worcester Watch Committee in December 1907 deferred judgement on making regulations because it would put the theatre authorities to considerable expense.[8]

The Barnsley Cinematograph accident in January 1908 forced many councils to look to their regulations for performances where children were present. The proprietors at this seasonal show were distributing sweets and gifts to children as they filed onto the stage. Youngsters in the gallery obviously fearing that they might miss out on this distribution rushed down the stairs. Some fell and others piled on top of them. Sixteen children were crushed to death in an accident that had nothing to do with the cinematograph but much to do with poor supervision.[9] As a reaction to this tragedy, the *Children's Act* of 1908 was rapidly placed on the Statute Book. It was the first Parliamentary Act aimed at cinematograph regulation. It required places of enter-

Some had argued that regulation would incur more expenses. Reynolds considered that this was a pluspoint, since it was the last thing 'rapacious penny gaff owners', would want to happen, and they would be put out of business.

From time to time, both *The Bioscope* and *The Kinematograph and Lantern Weekly* reported on the extent to which councils other than London had imposed regulations. The results, as would be expected, were patchy. For example, in October 1907, Middlesbrough Watch Committee empowered the Chief Constable to inspect licensed premises and ordered that exhibitors should give

tainment at which a majority of the persons attending were children, and where the child audience exceeded 100, to employ sufficient staff to control the movement of the children, before, during, and after the performance. Informants could earn £10 for passing the information of wrongdoing to the proper authority and acting as prosecution witnesses. Prosecutions under the Act were widely reported in both *The Bioscope* and *The Kinematograph and Lantern Weekly*. One such prosecution in Middlesbrough at the end of September 1909 seems to have been a fairly blatant case of profiteering. Despite the fact that the hall was full,

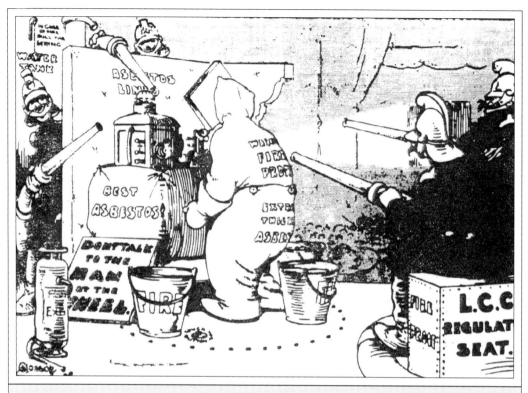

Fig. 3. 'The Safety of the Operator. Our idea of what will happen when the New Regulations come into force on 1 August.' From *The Bioscope*, 6 May 1909.

the son of the licensee continued to issue tickets and by the time the performance started all the gangways were partially or wholly blocked by children sitting on the floor. Moreover, there were insufficient adults to control movement. The Magistrates were lenient for this first offence, only fining Thomas Thompson £25 rather than the maximum £100.

The Home Secretary, Mr Gladstone, in March 1908 had demonstrated his intention to introduce a Bill regulating cinematograph performances but little progress seems to have been made on it during the year.[11] At the same time, The Royal Insurance Company issued a well-designed showcase for display in cinematograph halls. Its displayed clauses were almost a word-for-word repetition of the LCC regulations.

A number of projector fires occurred both in London and the provinces during the year, although none were reported to have got out of control. By January 1909, pressure on Mr Gladstone to introduce some form of legislation had increased. Mr Walter Reynolds of the LCC was now using the

phrase 'dangerous bioscope entertainments' to amplify his concern.[12] Faversham Council echoed the phrase when they looked at the extent of their regulations.[13] More and more councils considered their own local controls, and their deliberations were reported over the next few months in the cinema trade papers. Bath, Bradford, Dover, Sheffield, Wolverhampton and Wandsworth and most other London boroughs accepted the LCC regulations with little alteration. Aberdeen, Belfast, Birmingham, Bolton, Dublin, Glasgow, Hull, Leicester and Worcester indicated that they had no special regulations, except those applying to the inspection of all public buildings. Burton-on-Trent and Newcastle-upon-Tyne authorised the approved siting of projectors and lamphouses. Bristol, Burnley, Liverpool, Northampton, Nottingham, Paisley, Preston, Southport and Walsall required projectors to be placed in fireproof booths.

In February 1909, a brief press announcement indicated that a short Bill would be introduced to Parliament in the current session.[14] The occasion

Fig. 4. 'Arrival of the Cinematograph Bill. Consternation amongst Penny Showmen.' From *The Bioscope*, 13 May 1909.

again prompted the *Kinematograph Weekly* to interview Walter Reynolds on the possible scope of the regulations. He stated that it was not the desire of the London County Council to harm the legitimate business of the 'living picture man', but it was their desire to protect the public from danger. Since the first LCC regulation had been brought in there had only been twelve accidents in premises licensed by them. None of these incidents could be called serious.

One extra note, which was to have repercussions later, was presented by Mr Reynolds when he answered a question put to him by *The Kinematograph Weekly* interviewer about the control of the nature of the entertainments to be given. 'It is the duty of the police to stop any entertainment of doubtful character', he said, 'but certainly the Council would have the power, when licences came up for renewal, to refuse them to places that had presented undesirable shows'.[15]

First news of the contents of the Cinematograph Bill were published in the 1 April edition of *The Kinematograph and Lantern Weekly*. Its full title was 'A Bill to make better provision for securing safety at cinematograph and other entertainments'. The first clause regulated the exhibition of inflammable film to places complying with the regulations contained in the Bill. Licences for premises would be granted and renewed annually by the authority of county councils. Fines up to £20 could be given and an additional £5 for each day that premises continued to be used in contravention of the Act. Constables or appointed officers would have the right of entry. The Act did not apply to exhibitions in private dwelling houses. For occasional use in public premises, a licence would not be needed if seven days notice had been given to the authorities. It was envisaged that the *Cinematograph Act 1909* would come into operation on 1 August 1909. It seemed that this would give it ample time to receive its various readings and debates within the House of Commons and the House of Lords and to be examined and honed in its Committee stages. It was not

Fig. 5. 'Most of the showmen in this country are so busy turning the handle, counting the money – and sleeping – that the Cinematograph Bill is passing through unnoticed'. From *The Bioscope* 2 September 1909.

a contentious Bill and it was certain to receive cross-party support.

The complete Bill when published in the next editions of both *The Bioscope* and *The Kine Weekly* seemed to provide no major shocks for the trade. 'Only the "mere dabbler" or "the casual speculator" would be affected, and the trade had no need for them', stated *The Bioscope*.[16] Notwithstanding the publication of the Bill, which in almost all respects reflected its own views on safety, the LCC in the same week unilaterally drew up a new set of regulations for its own theatres. They were more specific than those in the Bill especially in defining such items as the thickness of the protecting metal plates in the projection booths.[17]

Press reports, as selected by *The Bioscope*, welcomed the timely intervention of Parliament into the safe presentation of this new, popular and inexpensive entertainment, especially since it was a form of entertainment that attracted large audiences of children.[18] The trade press picked up the point

that non-inflammable film shows did not require a licence. As to the question of censorship, a Bioscope barrister in discussing all the clauses of the Cinematograph Bill declared that this factor was covered by the Parliamentary Act 2 and 3 Victoria clause 47 section 54, sub-section 12 which stated that:

> It is an offence to exhibit any profane, indecent or obscene representation or to sing any profane indecent or obscene song or ballad to the annoyance of inhabitants or passengers.[19]

Travelling showmen felt particularly threatened by the Bill, and the Showmen's Guild met at the end of April to discuss the implications. Their main concern hinged on the use of the word 'premises'. Did this apply to portable structures such as tents? The Guild decided to seek clarification from the Home Secretary, since they felt that the regulations for permanent structures were unreasonable for portable ones. Eventually in September 1909, the Home Secretary agreed to some amendments to the application of the Bill to fairground travelling shows. It was conceded that the showman should be licensed by the authority in which he had a permanent address or residence. It was also agreed that travelling showmen in this circumstance should only need to give two days, notice instead of fourteen for setting up a cinematograph booth. They also had managed to insert a sub-section in the clause relating to the licensing of buildings for occasional use. This could now be extended from two days to six days per annum provided notice had been given to both the county council and the police.[20] In 1910, after the Act had come into force, a number of travelling showmen, either in ignorance or in confusion, failed to comply with the provisions of these amendments and are reported as being successfully prosecuted.

A small number of letters in the trade press warned against complacency in allowing the Bill to become law without a proper study of its implications. One letter, for example, read: 'No united action has been taken on these matters. When it is too late we shall all awake to the fact that legislation referring to any trade means less freedom of action and many tribulations, especially to smaller men.'[21]

The Bill's passage through Parliament was certainly much slower than anticipated and it was not put before the House of Lords for a first reading until September 1909, even though it had been largely unaltered since its first reading in the Commons.[22] During its passage through the Commons, an attempt had been made to bring non-inflammable films under its jurisdiction, but the amendment was, with agreement, withdrawn.[23]

While the Bill was with the Lords, the trade were alarmed by the activities of common informers causing prosecutions to be brought against cinematograph halls not possessing a music licence. They were rewarded with an informants fee of £10. The dilemma was that if they applied for a licence, their apparatus and projection room would need to conform to the regulations for theatres. With the passage of the *Cinematograph Act*, this contradiction would be removed, and although the Act made no mention of music, it was clearly in the best interest of the proprietors that they should apply for music licences along with their cinematograph licence.[24]

A worrying sign that the placing of enforcement of the *Cinematograph Act* regulations in the

hands of local licensing authorities would lead to excessive harassment of exhibitors appeared in the actions of Sheffield Council. They produced local regulations that required the attendance of a trained fireman at all performances at a cost of 30 shillings per week, and the establishment of a direct telephone line between the operator's box and the local firestation. F.S. Mottershaw of The Sheffield Photo Company protested his safe use of a portable fire-proof box in vain.[25]

The first of January 1910 was the operational date for the Act. *The Bioscope* was mostly satisfied with its clauses and its mode of application. Like it or not, the film industry now had to face the fact that its exhibition side was to undergo statutory regulation for the first time. It was also clear that this regulation might constitute a control of the content of the films being exhibited and, by reverse extrapolation, control of the content of films that were being made *for* exhibition. Moreover, the cinematograph licence itself could define the opening and closing hours of each venue, and, by extension, indicate the operational days of the week. Sunday opening was only one area of contention. Good Friday and Christmas day were also seen to be traditional days of rest from work and 'entertainment'.

A wide variety of different committees were proposed as the licensing authorities, but there seemed to be little to choose between them in their function. *The Bioscope* during January and February 1910 reported the diversity. For example, Kent and Suffolk were regulated directly by the county council. Surrey delegated its powers to the Music and Dance Committee. The City of Bristol and the County of Wiltshire gave their powers to the Sanitary Committee. Burton-on-Trent employed their General Purposes Committee. Barrow, Colchester, Derby, Durham The Isle of White, Rutland and Somerset and the majority of other Councils extended the powers of the existing magistrate and police courts which annually renewed the licences of public houses, theatres, roller-skating rinks and dance halls. Blackpool, Exeter, Kendal, Leicester, Reading and Wigan along with numerous others entrusted the task to their existing Watch Committees.

In London, the first prosecution under the Act was not long in appearing. The G.L. Syndicate, who were occupiers of The Royal Cambridge Music Hall in Commercial Street, Spitalfields, were summoned for allowing the premises to be used on four different days in January without obtaining a licence. The proprietors had been given notice that they would be in contravention of the Act if they did not make their equipment comply with regulations. They were using electric current at 480 volts instead of the 110 volts required by the Act. In their defence the proprietors said that they were using 480 volts because that was the voltage supplied by the electricity station owned by the borough council. Although a new transformer had been installed by the time the case came to court, the magistrates found the company guilty of deliberately breaking the law, and fined them £20 for the first day and £4 for each of the other three days. The total fine including costs amounted to £33 and 1 shilling (£33.5p).[26]

Not all contraventions resulted in court appearances and fines. A film show for the Richmond Branch of the National Anti-Vivisection Association was merely halted by the police because insufficient notice had been given of the performance.[27]

On 6 January, at a meeting in Holborn of cinematograph proprietors and traders, it was decided to form a Defence League to protect themselves from over-zealous councils in the implementation of the Act. Among other things, they took exception to the fact that the Cinematograph Act was being used as a Sunday Closing Act. The Bioscope saw this as discrimination against the poor. The rich in their clubs could find amusement on a Sunday night. The toiling masses and the poor could not.[28]

Some minor sections of the Act such as the regulation size of take-up spools, demonstrated a certain lack of knowledge of the actual technology of film projection by some parliamentary advisers. It was stipulated that the bottom spool should be 12 inches (334 mm) in diameter or 14 inches (358 mm) when only one film was being projected. The trade was quick to point out that this implied that a 100-foot film had to be taken up on a 14-inch spool, whereas a 1000-foot top spool containing several films had to be squeezed onto a 12-inch take-up spool.[29]

The exact status of the Cinematograph Act was demonstrated in February when the London County Council issued its own regulations under the delegation permitted by the Act. The most important

change was, as forecast, the enforcement of a Sunday closing regulation. This was open to appeal if the show was being given in aid of charity.[30] It was also restated that cinemas would need a music licence if they used accompanying music.

The Defence League, however, did have some success with the Home Secretary, and on 18 February, the spool size and the incoming voltage regulations were sufficiently altered, along with some other clauses, to be more in keeping with common practice. Mr Gladstone made it clear that the original spool regulation was intended to prevent the films from 'projecting beyond the edges of the flanges of the spool'.[31]

During 1910, there were many more instances of buildings being reported as unsuitable for cinematograph projection, but whether this was because of the existence of the Cinematograph Act or because it was now more newsworthy for The Bioscope and The Kinematograph Weekly to report them, is not clear. A news item in The Bioscope of 17 November 1910 claimed that 20 per cent of applications for cinematograph licences to the LCC failed to comply with the regulations of the Act or their own.

Travelling showmen had managed to persuade the Home Secretary to amend the regulations in March 1910, so that the word 'booth' was included as well as 'building' when applied to the rules about the operational venue,[32] but they were still the most vulnerable group of the Act's victims. Typical of the cases brought before the magistrates' courts is that of showman Edward A. Francis. He was charged at Gilling East in Yorkshire with giving a cinematograph performance without having notified the chief constable of the North Riding. He said that he did not think that he needed one because he had got one from the chief constable of Durham when he had given a show at Trimdon Grange in that county. The magistrates informed him that he needed a licence for every village to which he went, but as they thought the defendant might genuinely have been misled by the regulations, they would treat him leniently and only fine him £1 including court costs.[33]

By the end of 1910, though, it was the opinion of The Bioscope that the regulations and the resulting trade activity had consolidated the industry and given it an increased standing in its own eyes and in the eyes of the public.[34] The initial impetus for nationally applied regulations had been for the physical safety of patrons of moving picture shows. The film trade, for the most part, had been self-regulating in this respect for some years, and co-operation with local regulatory bodies was almost universal. In many quarters it was felt that well-thought-through national regulations would both assist this partnership and protect showmen from local authorities or pressure groups perceived to be over-zealous and antagonistic.

In the event, The Royal Assent to the 1909 *Cinematograph Act* and its 1 January application in 1910 hardly rated a mention in most newspapers. Where mention was made, there was unanimous approval of the safety aspects. The 1909 *Cinematograph Act* remained in force until it was replaced by the 1952 *Cinematograph Act*. By this time, the use of inflammable cinematograph film had been almost completely discontinued, and the title was amended to 'An Act to make better provision for the *regulating* of Cinematograph and other exhibitions' (my italics). The net result of the original *Cinematograph Act*, then, was the opportunity it afforded local authorities to strengthen their regulation of the content of programmes, a factor not originally intended by the legislation, but which in later years became its *raison d'être*.○

Notes.

1. Supplement to *The Bioscope* (23 December 1909).

2. *Kinematograph* and *Lantern Weekly*, (K.W.) (12 September 1907).

3. Before the establishment of the National Grid in Great Britain in 1926, the supply of electricity was chaotic. In London alone, there were 50 different systems with 20 different voltages and 10 different frequencies.

4. *K.W.* (12 November 1908).

5. *K.W.* (4 December 1908).

6. *K.W.* (17 December 1908).

7. *K.W.* (17 October 1907).

8. *K.W.* (26 December 1907).

9. *K.W.* (16 January 1908).

10. *The Bioscope* (23 September 1909).

11. *K.W.* (5 March 1908).

12. *The Bioscope* (28 January 1909).

13. *K.W.* (18 March 1909).

14. *K.W.* (11 February 1909).

15. *Ibid.*

16. *The Bioscope* (1 April 1909).

17. *The Bioscope* (8 April 1909).

18. *Ibid.*

19. *The Bioscope* (29 April 1909).

20. *The Bioscope* (29 April 1909, 30 September 1909, 21 October 1909).

21. *The Bioscope* (24 June 1909). Part of a letter from Stebbings and Edwards of London.

22. *The Bioscope* (23 September 1909).

23. *The Bioscope* (16 September 1909).

24. *The Bioscope* (2 December 1909).

25. *The Bioscope* (14 October 1909).

26. *The Bioscope* (27 January 1910).

27. *The Bioscope* (17 February 1910).

28. The Bioscope (6 January 1910).

29. *Ibid.*

30. *The Bioscope* (3 February 1910). The question of Sunday opening dogged the industry for another 50 years. The arguments, defining by-laws and regulations, are the subject of a separate study by myself as they relate to my current researches into 'The Cinema in a Cathedral City'.

31. *The Bioscope* (3 March 1910).

32. The *Music Hall and Theatre Review* (19 March 1910).

33. *The Bioscope* (14 July 1910).

34. *The Bioscope* (29 December 1910).

Film History, Volume 9, pp. 351–364, 1997. Copyright © John Libbey & Company
ISSN: 0892-2160. Printed in Australia

'Oil upon the flames of vice': The battle over white slave films in New York City

Shelley Stamp Lindsey

The "white slave pictures" have again this week occupied the whole attention of the show business. There has been no end to the talk, comment and arguments over them,'[1] *Variety* announced in the third week of December 1913, when two infamous films on the already sensationalised topic of white slavery dominated New York screens.

At a time when Chicago had become the locus of white slave panic following its alarmist 1911 report on the 'social evil',[2] New York emerged as the centre of controversy surrounding cinematic depictions of the slave trade. It was in New York that the films were initially released, there that they began attracting phenomenal crowds, and there that they first generated controversy. The battle over white slave films was staged in the city's courts, in its daily papers where the controversy was front-page news, in the New York-based industry trade journals, in publications of the progressive reform movement, and finally at the box office where crowds amassing at theatres along Broadway fought to see the pictures everyone was talking about. Several factions figure in this debate, each vying to exercise control over motion picture exhibition in Manhattan: the city's police force, testing the application of obscenity laws to film screenings; the city's reform community, very much divided on mat-

ters of the cinema; the city's film industry, still reeling from Nickelodeon closings five years earlier and keenly invested in efforts to uplift the cinema; and finally the National Board of Censorship of Motion Pictures, determined to exert its influence over film exhibition at a time when calls for state and federal censorship were gathering strength.[3]

The first of the white slave films, *Traffic in Souls* (Independent Moving Picture Co.), was a hit the day it opened in New York on 24 November 1913, where it played to three packed houses at Joe Weber's Theater on Broadway at 29th Street, despite the 25-cent tickets.[4] Film-goers promised a 'two hour' show by this six-reel feature were evidently willing to pay the high price of admission. With nearly 1000 seats, Weber's was triple the capacity of most motion picture venues in the city.[5] When *The Inside of the White Slave Traffic* (Moral Feature Film Co.) opened a week later at the 1800-seat Park Theater on Columbus Circle, several hundred

Shelley Stamp Lindsey is Assistant Professor of film and video at the University of California, Santa Cruz, CA. Her study of women and motion picture culture in the 1910s will be published by Princeton University Press. Correspondence to: Film and Video, Porter College, University of California, Santa Cruz, CA 95064, USA.

people had to be turned away, the majority of whom were young women.[6] By the fourth week of December both films played simultaneously on two screens in New York. *The Inside of the White Slave Traffic* offered five additional daily showings at the Bijou Theater on Broadway, just one block north of Weber's where *Traffic in Souls* continued to play. Further uptown, police were called in to manage crowds when *Traffic in Souls* opened additional showings at the Republic Theater.[7] Within less than a month of its opening, *Traffic in Souls* was playing simultaneously at six theatres in greater New York to no less enthusiastic audiences. At the height of their success in New York, *Traffic in Souls* and *The Inside of the White Slave Traffic* generated close to $5000 apiece in weekly box office grosses, suggesting that upwards of 15,000 New Yorkers saw the pictures each week.[8]

With *Traffic in Souls* and *The Inside of the White Slave Traffic* doing so well, rival New York exhibitors complained that vice pictures were cutting into their receipts. Dozens of production companies across the country, eager to capitalise on the craze, reportedly had white slave films in the works.[9] 'They are coming thick and fast', the *New York Clipper* reported.[10] So furious was the competition for audiences that makers of *The Inside of the White Slave Traffic* threatened to seek an injunction against any other production using the term 'white slave' in its title, claiming sole copyright.[11] Nonetheless, imitators were so readily available that exhibitors eager to prolong the bankability of vice themes frequently replaced one white slave title with another. When the Bijou Theater abandoned trouble-plagued screenings of *The Inside of the White Slave Traffic* in the last week of December, they immediately replaced it with *The Exposure of the White Slave Traffic* (A + A Inc.), a cheaply made English film that had been released in theatres on the lower East Side and Harlem three years earlier. Following the popularity of white slave pictures at relatively upscale Broadway theatres, owners of the Bijou resurrected *The Exposure of the White Slave Traffic*, adding additional still pictures and a lecturer, and billing it as 'The European Version of the White Slave Traffic'. The formula appeared to work, for *Variety* reported that 'the picture did business from the outset and had a crowd waiting to gain entrance by one o'clock' on its first day, despite

management's decision to double admission prices for its run.[12] So popular was this newcomer that it threatened *Traffic in Souls*, still playing at Weber's one block south. '"Slave" Beating "Souls"', screamed *Variety* as it chronicled the battle for the box office.[13] After a three-week run, the Bijou replaced *The Exposure of the White Slave Traffic* with *The House of Bondage* (Photo Drama Motion Picture Co.), a screen adaptation of Reginald Wright Kauffman's wildly popular 1910 novel, by then in its fourteenth edition. The film had been rushed into production in December and was released while a stage version of Kauffman's work still played in New York, a unprecedented occurrence.[14] *Traffic in Souls* ended its startling eight-week run at Weber's with declining box office receipts and was itself finally replaced by a cheaply and quickly made imitator *Smashing the Vice Trust* (Progress Film Co.) in late January.[15]

The vice film sensation was ultimately short-lived. In less than two months the white slave theme was so familiar that it invited parody in the spoof *Traffickers in Soles* (Feature Photoplay Co.), which adhered closely to the 'regulation "vice" plot', according to *Motion Picture News*.[16] By early February *Moving Picture World* would report 'happily the hysteria is rapidly passing away and we are even in New York City returning to sane and normal conditions.'[17] While it lasted, however, the storm of controversy that gathered around the 'slavers' tells us a great deal about the new role that socially conscious films were playing in urban culture, and the struggle over motion picture exhibition in cities across the country as film became the nation's premiere entertainment form. Did feature-length white slave films herald cinema's final descent into tawdry cheap amusements? Or did they mark a point of maturity when the cinema might be able to shed light upon society's most troublesome social problems?

Confirmation that white slave films became synonymous with the larger evils of cinema at this key moment can be found in a cartoon published in the *New York Sun* at the height of the controversy.[18] Entitled 'The Movie', the cartoon depicts a man and woman purchasing tickets for a film called 'The White Slave'. Although a small notice on the ticket booth proclaims the show 'a great moral lesson for young and old', the overwhelming architecture of the Medusa Theatre seems to contradict this view. The Medusa's head that shapes the theatre's exterior is, of course, reminiscent of the ornate, quasi-classical façades and plasters that increasingly adorned motion picture houses in these years. But, in this figuration, the theatre entrance becomes an engulfing orifice, a visual echo of the wide, wild eyes and gapping, screaming mouth of the Medusa pictured at the top of the frame. In this view the cinema, epitomised by the white slave pictures, becomes a horror too terrifying to view.

New Yorkers drawn to the films could scarcely have escaped sensational details about the city's supposed white slave trade widely circulating in the press long before the films were released. Local panic escalated sharply in 1909 when *McClure's* magazine published an exposé of vice trafficking and police corruption in Manhattan penned by muckraker George Kibbe Turner. 'New York has become the leader of the world' in slave trafficking, Turner alleged, the conduit through which immigrant traffickers entered the country and out of which women were shipped around the nation and worldwide.[19] All this was tacitly condoned by the Democratic political machine at Tammany Hall, he claimed. Picking up on Turner's charges, headlines in the *New York Times* warned 'There Is a White Slave Traffic' and advised readers 'White Slave Traffic Shown to Be Real'.[20] So grave were Turner's allegations that white slavery became the topic of municipal elections that fall. A special Grand Jury was formed to investigate Turner's charges early in 1910, headed by Standard Oil scion and eager do-gooder, John D. Rockefeller, Jr. The arrest in May of slave traffickers who had sold women to undercover Grand Jury investigators only fuelled the panic. However, the Grand Jury's detailed report, made public in June, ultimately concluded there was little evidence of an organised traffic in women,

Fig. 1. 'The Movie', *New York Sun*, 29 December 1913.

despite Turner's appearance as star witness.[21] Following his Grand Jury service, an undaunted Rockefeller founded the Bureau of Social Hygiene to investigate conditions of prostitution and white slavery in the city more thoroughly. That summer the Bureau issued its first study, George Kneeland's *Commercialised Prostitution in New York City*. Famed for his investigations for the Chicago Vice Commission, Kneeland warned readers that New York's slave ring procurers lurked 'wherever girls congregate for business or pleasure' ready to snatch innocent victims.[22] In the months following Kneeland's report and leading up to the films' release, the city's daily papers were rife with accounts of women being abducted by white slavers, sexually assaulted by 'mashers', or stabbed with poison needles. The front-page coverage often accorded these stories seemed to prove that women were in grievous danger on the streets of New York.

Coincident with Kneeland's report, two Broadway plays on the vice trade, *The Fight* and *The Lure*,

Fig. 2. 'We are the white slaves of the cinema', *New York World*, 17 January 1914.

also appeared in the late summer of 1913, barely three months before *Traffic in Souls* brought the theme to the screen.[23] New York newspapers condemned the 'brothel plays' for exposing the city's underworld before its well-heeled theatre-goers. 'Veiled thinly with the pretense of deploring the social evil, their real purpose is to hold it up to morbid eyes', claimed the *New York Times*.[24] In a lengthy analysis for the paper's Sunday edition, famed Harvard psychologist, and later film theorist, Hugo Münsterberg argued in great detail that the presentation of such themes on the stage, in what he called a 'black frame about a living picture', did more harm than good. Matters of sexual deviance were better left unspoken, he maintained.[25] Rising criticism in the city's newspapers prompted police scrutiny of both productions. Producers were summoned to appear before New York's chief police magistrate and revisions were demanded of *The Fight*.[26] Sensational coverage also attended a police raid upon the stage production of *The House of Bondage* after it opened in December and popular actress Cecil Spooner, the play's star, was arrested in her dressing room prior to the second evening's performance.[27] Police attention ultimately had a contradictory effect on Broadway. The intense police scrutiny of *The Lure* and blow-by-blow coverage in the city's newspapers only added to the productions' popularity, resulting in overflow crowds at each performance. Just one month before the release of *Traffic in Souls*, *Moving Picture World*

condemned the productions, suggesting they were merely a 'last desperate expedient to draw audiences away from the motion picture theatres. Instead of attracting the crowds, they have succeeded in attracting the police'.[28]

Concerns raised about the stage productions anticipated those that would resurface in the even more contentious debate over film versions of the same material later than autumn: did dramatisations of the slave trade perform an educational service in exposing hitherto unseen aspects of the urban underworld, or did they simply cater to prurient interests?; who ought to see such productions, if they did indeed hold educational merit?; and should official censorship be brought to bear upon artistic works, and in whose hands should the power of decision-making rest? Attendant to the larger implications of police censorship, the *New York Dramatic Mirror* wondered 'whether the New York police department is intellectually or morally fit to say whether a play shall be produced'.[29] Unlike other contemporary inscriptions of white slavery, stage plays raised particularly troubling issues because of their visual enactment of scenes of prostitution and sexual behavior. As the *Mirror* suggested, audiences for such productions were 'vicariously visiting a low resort and seeing the inner life of the underworld from a new angle of view'.[30] These were precisely the issues that would resurface even more insistently in the debate over white slavery on screen.

White slave films announced cinema's 'arrival' as a major entertainment form in New York with particular force, for they helped to dramatise the wide-spread conversion of 'legitimate' theatres into moving picture houses in the early 1910s. Many of New York's top-ranked Broadway playhouses, including Weber's and the Republic where *Traffic in Souls* played, made the transition to motion picture exhibition with so-called 'vicers'.[31] Fifteen major theatres had 'gone into film slavery' by early 1914, according to the *New York World*, suggesting that the trope of sexual slavery came to symbolise the relationship between theatre and motion pictures as a whole. The paper's comic illustration showed a new Broadway landscape now dominated by lurid movie marquees of violent traffickers and their pitiable victims. Traditional advocates of the theatre were particularly unsettled. Oscar Hammerstein, owner of the Republic Theater, threatened suit against leasee David Belasco for subleasing the theatre to Universal during the run of *Traffic in Souls*, claiming that such 'indecent' fare contravened Belasco's contract to stage 'first class productions', then he threatened to prevent Belasco from exhibiting motion pictures at the Republic altogether.[32] Though ultimately unsuccessful, Hammerstein's lawsuit suggests how anxieties surrounding competition between movies and stage plays crystallised around the white slave films, and how the trend allowed critics to paint the conversion of theatres in very dire terms. 'We are the white slaves of the cinema', cried the *New York World*, ' ... for, like the tango, the movies have strangled the stage in every land and clime'.[33]

Large Broadway theatres relatively new to the movie trade and willing to charge 25 cents for feature film admissions, were also willing to adver-

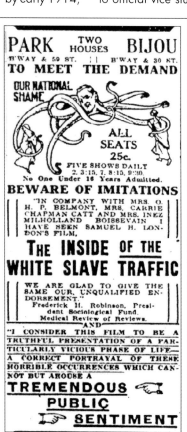

Fig. 3. Advertisement, *New York Tribune*, December 1913.

tise on Sunday newspaper pages normally reserved for stage productions.[34] *Traffic in Souls, The Inside of the White Slave Traffic*, and *Smashing the Vice Trust* were, it appears, the only films advertised in New York's daily papers in late 1913 and early 1914. New Yorkers who followed the city's vice scare in the daily papers would no doubt have seen film adaptations of the white slave theme advertised there as well. Adverts touted erroneous connections to official vice studies and boasted endorsements from respected civic leaders. *The Inside of the White Slave Traffic* was 'produced from actual facts'[35] and 'based on the actual observations of a former US government investigator',[36] according to its publicity, while *Smashing the Vice Trust* was actually 'based on District Attorney Whitman's disclosures'.[37] *Traffic in Souls* professed to be 'the only true and authentic version' of the traffic in women, 'the only production that has the endorsement and sanction of the many vice crusaders throughout the country'.[38] If these claims seem designed to highlight the films' educational merits, simultaneous promises of visual splendor unmistakably link this verisimilitude to sexual explicitness: *Traffic in Souls* promised viewers 'a two hour show depicting graphically the evils of the white slave traffic';[39] *Smashing the Vice Trust*, 'a heart-rending spectacle in six parts and 700 scenes';[40] and *The Inside of the White Slave Traffic*, 'A film with a moral. A film with a lesson. A film with a thrill'.[41] Cloaking the films' treatment of sexual material in terms of visual spectacle, these ads suggest that film versions of the slave trade offered what no other medium could: an actual glimpse into the city's brothels and red-light districts.

Not surprisingly, it was just this aspect of the films that attracted police attention in New York

Fig. 4. Advertisement, *New York Tribune,* February 1914.

where The *The Inside of the White Slave Traffic* enjoyed a particularly rocky run. *Variety* was quick to predict that the film would incur police censorship, given its portrayal of 'the same scene that brought the police down upon two red-light dramas and howling crowds to the box office'[42] earlier that autumn. *Traffic in Souls,* the paper predicted, 'may escape police censorship here and elsewhere because it omits the soul of a subject it aims to reveal', whereas its racier counterpart risked the censor's knife since it 'goes in for the utmost fidelity in picturing the evil which has been its inspiration'.[43]

As predicted, the Park Theater's manager was summoned to police court during the second week of the film's engagement to answer charges that *The Inside of the White Slave Traffic* constituted an immoral and indecent exhibition. After a police magistrate viewed the film and heard testimony on the film's behalf from several of the city's notable social reformers, the complaint was dismissed.[44] But the headline in the *New York Press* the next morning screamed, 'Police Can't Stop White Slave Film. Lose Step In Fight to Check Vice and Sex Hysteria Sweeping City'.[45] Evidently unsatisfied with the magistrate's decision, the Deputy Police Commissioner secured a warrant for the arrest of Samuel London,

the film's producer, on the grounds that the film was 'calculated to harm the morals of young people'. Police raided the Park Theater on Friday evening of that same week, bringing with them a volume of officers and patrol wagons more suited to a raid on a gambling joint than a movie house, according to one observer, but failed to arrest London who was not on the premises.[46] When the Park Theater resumed showing *The Inside of the White Slave Traffic* the very next day, police again raided the theatre in mid-afternoon while a screening was in progress. This time officers arrested all of the Park's employees – manager, ticket seller, ticket taker, and projectionist – and confiscated the film print. According to the *New York Sun*'s colourful account, an officer stood in the projection booth grabbing each of the five reels as it came off the projector. At midnight theatre management announced to waiting crowds that a temporary injunction had been obtained preventing further police interference, and that screenings would resume the following afternoon.[47]

Two successive police raids on the Park the weekend before Christmas drew intense public interest in *The Inside of the White Slave Traffic.* The raids were front-page news in virtually all of New York's dailies. 'Slave Reel Spins; Police Hands

Tied', cried the *Tribune*. This attention generated intense public interest in the film, an appetite to which owners of the Park Theater readily catered. The day following the second raid, the Park offered eight showings of *The Inside of the White Slave Traffic* instead of its usual five, using duplicate prints of the confiscated material and brazenly adding a fifth reel to the show despite the presence of police officers outside the theatre. Crowds began gathering early in the afternoon, a full hour before management announced that screenings would begin.[48] 'The advertising the so-called white slave films have been given through the efforts of the police to suppress them has resulted in extraordinary attendance at the Park Theatre', the *New York World* reported. Such attention 'brought a crowd of fully five thousand men, women and children into Columbus Circle' that afternoon, according to the *Herald*, with the *Tribune* reporting 'crowds surging in and out of the doors of the theatre in increasing volumes with each succeeding exhibition'.[49]

By Monday a second set of daily screenings was offered at the Bijou Theater, further down Broadway at 30th street, in order to accommodate audience demand. Temporarily prevented from interfering with screenings at the Park, police raided the Bijou on the second night of the film's run there, after receiving a warrant from a magistrate vowing to stem the 'riot of obscene spectacles that is going on in our city'. But again management obtained a temporary injunction preventing police interference.[50] Large crowds continued to attend both the Park and the Bijou all week, reportedly drawing the biggest business the film had seen since it opened.[51] In fact, front-page coverage of the police raids was thought to explain the temporary drop in attendance at *Traffic in Souls* still playing one block south of the Bijou at Weber's and uptown at the Republic.[52]

By the last week of December, however, temporary injunctions preventing police interference at both the Park and Bijou were vacated, giving police authorities full license to suspend the productions, which they did.[53] *The Inside of the White Slave Traffic* quickly disappeared from New York screens before the end of December, within less than a month of its opening. When Samuel London, his manager and the manager of the Bijou were eventually convicted of exhibiting material 'tending to

corrupt the morals' at a closely watched March trial, the New York Herald declared, 'the happy result is that [*The Inside of the White Slave Traffic*] never can be shown again in any theatre in this city, and it is not likely other cities will take what New York has condemned'.[54]

Film industry leaders were justifiably alarmed by the specter of police repeatedly raiding New York movie theatres the week before Christmas, exactly five years after common show licences had been revoked by Mayor McClellan in 1908. Indeed, the trouble-plagued run of *The Inside of the White Slave Traffic* highlighted still-lingering struggles over motion picture exhibition in Manhattan. Just five months earlier the city had finally passed an ordinance governing its movie theatres, after more than two years of contentious debate initiated by newly elected mayor, William Gaynor, who favoured liberalising licensing laws that had restricted the growth of motion picture venues in the past. In the wake of the 1908 closings, many of the city's alderman favoured an ordinance that would regulate film *content* as well as theatrical space, hoping to establish a police censorship board similar to one that had been operating in Chicago since 1907. Gaynor, a staunch opponent of municipal censorship, vetoed two motion picture ordinances in 1912 and 1913 that included censorship provisions, arguing that public outrage, coupled with already existing obscenity laws, were sufficient to prevent the exhibition of indecent material on the city's screens. The final ordinance, signed by Gaynor in July of 1913, explicitly refused municipal censorship.[55] Following closely upon the heels of this tumultuous debate then, white slave films once again opened discussions about how the cinema ought to be regulated in New York.

The *New York Dramatic Mirror*, *Variety*, and *Moving Picture World* all issued strong and repeated condemnations of the films, claiming 'they are all bad, not alone for the public, but for the moving picture industry'.[56] Vice pictures were 'a danger to the business' that would 'lower the esteem in which film plays are held' and 'lessen respect for moving pictures wherever exhibited'.[57] Many of the city's exhibitors and film producers called upon the mayor and the police to suspend exhibitions of *The Inside of the White Slave Traffic*.[58] In January, with *Traffic in Souls* still playing, the All-Star Feature

Corporation published an open letter to Universal-head Carl Laemmle in New York's Sunday papers. 'In the name of the twenty-five million Americans who depend on the motion picture for their daily relaxation', the letter declared, 'we protest against your company's appeal … to those bestial instincts which are the rebellious and destructive elements in our social life'.[59]

Particularly worrisome were fears that sensational coverage of police raids in New York 'stirred up the imps of censorship', as W. Stephen Bush put it, at a time when calls for state and municipal censorship were gaining strength.[60] Bush, who fought tirelessly against censorship during his tenure at *Moving Picture World*, actually endorsed police intervention in the exhibition of such films, arguing that existing obscenity laws could sufficiently contain vice pictures without official censorship.[61] The *New York Dramatic Mirror* feared that 'when the small-city press and the small-city pulpits get their say, then the few victories that have been won in the fight to ward off local censorship will have to be fought all over again, with a strong weapon placed in the hands of the agitators'.[62]

Louis Reeves Harrison, in two *Moving Picture World* editorials on the films, must have echoed much of the industry's sentiments when he complained that vice pictures alienated the 'family' audience and risked sabotaging the industry's uplift.[63] In the end, though, Harrison maintained that agitation surrounding the vice pictures marked a 'step in the evolution of the New Art', since 'honest censorship and manly criticism' championed the cause of middle-class patrons, rather than alienating them. In short, by publicly castigating white slave films, the industry could stage its *own* uplift.

The police attention which *The Inside of the White Slave Traffic* garnered upon its New York release came exactly as Universal was preparing 40 prints of *Traffic in Souls* for national distribution and an aggressive campaign was promoting states' rights sales and direct booking of *The Inside of the White Slave Traffic*.[64] If anything, the vice films' notorious New York debut only added to their cachet. A trade ad describing 'the raging sensation in New York' boasted that exhibitors 'turned two thousand away the second night after the fourth show at the Park Theater'.[65] A two-page trade ad for *Smashing the Vice Trust* described the picture as

'the sensation of New York', and quoted from many of the New York press notices.[66]

The Inside of the White Slave Traffic later played several cities without incident – among them Trenton, New Jersey, Allentown, Pennsylvania, and Schenectady, New York – but in many cases the New York scrutiny prompted municipalities to ban the film, or shorten its run, on the principle that if the picture had been deemed unsuitable for New Yorkers, it must be wholly inappropriate for the rest of the country.[67] 'The New York police stopped it, and our police should never let it open here',[68] declared a Chicago alderman after viewing the film. 'If it's too bad for New York, it certainly should not be shown in Washington',[69] said that city's mayor. Exhibitors there and in Newark, New Jersey, cut runs of the film short because of police action against the production in New York.

Members of New York's reform community were more divided in their response to the white slave films. *The Inside of the White Slave Traffic*, in particular, caused 'a row among sociological workers', according to the *New York World*.[70] Many reformers questioned the wisdom of exposing the city's vice conditions in such a vivid, life-like manner to the movie-going public. John D. Rockefeller Jr. for his part took deliberate steps to dissociate himself from productions claiming to be based upon his work at the Bureau of Social Hygiene: 'I and those associated with me in this work regard this method of exploiting vice as not only injudicious but positively harmful', he claimed.[71] When the New York-based progressive monthly *The Outlook* published a January 1914 editorial that advocated the use of popular media like cinema to convey information on sensitive topics like prostitution, it was met by an unequivocally hostile response from readers who questioned the motives of viewers at such films.[72] Reports of *female* patrons attending the pictures shocked reformers even more profoundly, as I have argued elsewhere.[73] Speaking at the height of the controversy Rabbi Stephen S. Wise told an audience at the Free Synagogue in Carnegie Hall that despite cinema's educational potential, the current crop of white slave films did 'nothing more than stimulate an unwholesome and morbid curiosity instead of driving home a moral lesson'.[74] Even the *New York Times* entered the debate, arguing that films depicting white slavery only 'pour oil upon the flames of vice'.[75]

Yet, there was a growing constituency of New York-based social reformers eager to exploit the educational potential of cinema, and fearful of police control over censorship. As a result, *The Inside of the White Slave Traffic* received support from many prominent progressives.[76] Its title sequence carried endorsements from many notables, including Carrie Chapman Catt, Charlotte Perkins Gilman, People's Institute-head Frederic Howe, 'and many others, including every sociologist of note from Atlantic to Pacific'. Placards in the Bijou Theater's lobby also reminded film-goers of these endorsements.[77] The film's chief supporter was Fredrick Robinson, head of the Sociological Fund of the *Medical Review of Reviews*. He monitored raids on theatres where the film was shown and castigated police for suppressing the film, hoping the debate would 'determine once and for all time whether the police may constitute themselves the judges and censors in our community'.[78] Once it became clear that *The Inside of the White Slave Traffic* could not be shown commercially in the city without police interference, Robinson and several other supports vowed to conduct private screenings of the film, during which they also planned to distribute copies of Christabel Pankhurst's banned publication *Plain Facts About a Great Evil*.[79] 'The fight long ago moved out of the range of film news', declared the *New York Dramatic Mirror*, 'and became a struggle between those who want to publish … facts about the white slave traffic and the police'.[80]

Where was the National Board of Censorship amidst this controversy, one might well ask? Formed just four years earlier in an alliance between New York's reform community and its film industry chiefs, the Board had sought to prove that under the guidance of moral leadership filmmakers could regulate themselves without state intervention.[81] But the battle over vice pictures tested the authority of this fledgling alliance.

Board of Censorship records show that the organisation was acutely conscious of its role in judging the white slave films because of their particular mixture of avowedly educational content and relative sexual explicitness. When they reviewed *Traffic in Souls* in late October, nearly four weeks

prior to its release, Board members declared themselves fully aware that 'a precedent would be created by any action taken' since the picture dealt 'in a more deliberate and extensive way than any previous film with the so-called white slave traffic'.[82] Seeking perhaps to bolster their decision, the Board invited representatives of New York's reform community to view and discuss the film with the their own General Committee, soliciting their input on the propriety of treating vice themes through motion pictures, and the question of 'whether it is rightly within the province of the National Board of Censorship to interfere with such public discussions through motion pictures'.[83] After requesting five alterations that reduced scenes in brothel interiors and minimised suggestions that the slave ring leader was a reformer, the Board passed *Traffic in Souls*.[84] 'This subject and this method of treatment were legitimate in motion pictures', the Board declared, maintaining that the film was 'a high-grade picture capable of real moral and dramatic entertainment'.[85]

Board of Censorship approval clearly held currency in the industry at a time when white slave pictures were 'bound to arouse bitter antagonism', according to *Moving Picture World*. Noting that the 'work has been carefully reviewed by the censors' and that 'several eliminations have been made', the trade journal's review of *Traffic in Souls* openly touted the Board's sanction: 'Surely its friends, and among these are the members of the National Board of Censorship, are entitled to ask that the production be seen before it is condemned.'[86] White slavery was 'dealt with so reverently', according to the *Motion Picture News*, 'that even the members of the National Board of Censorship could not find fault' with *Traffic in Souls*.[87] *Motography*'s two-page review carried a headline announcing, 'Censors Have Indorsed It'.[88] Still, the latter trade viewed the Board's publicly issued justification of its ruling as a defensive gesture: 'the action of the Censor Board in issuing this advance explanation manifestly anticipates criticism from some source', *Motography* claimed, suggesting something of the Board's own uncertainty about its mandate.[89]

The Board's hesitancy in dealing with vice pictures, while evident in its handling of *Traffic in Souls*, was most apparent in its uneven treatment of *The Inside of the White Slave Traffic*. The Board screened the film when it opened in New York in the second week of December, voting to approve the picture with certain specified changes. This decision was never publicly released, however. Instead, fearing that producer Samuel London would exploit its approval for publicity purposes, the Board deemed *The Inside of the White Slave Traffic* a 'special release', a category that left censorship decisions up to local communities. Officially, the Board took 'no stand either for or against' the film. However, after pressure from London and the producer's written assurance that he would abide by the Board's judgment and not exploit a favourable ruling, the Board agreed to revisit the film two weeks after it had opened in New York. In order to receive the Board's sanction, London would have to eliminate footage shot in New Orleans' red-light district and trim scenes set inside brothels. Scenes showing the downfall of the female victim and the eventual punishment of the trafficker must also be added. The General Committee of the Board gathered at the Park Theater for a screening of a revised print of *The Inside of the White Slave Traffic* on Monday, 22 December, following the sensational weekend of double police raids. Although London had evidently added new material, the Board refused the pass the film, citing its sensationalistic title, its portrayal of brothel interiors, and its failure to vitiate the slave trade. It was, they declared, wholly unsuitable for popular audiences. In a statement released to the press that evening, committee members complained that 'the picture was distinctly an illustration of the white slave traffic, thinly veiled as an attempt to educate the public'.[90]

This episode seems indicative of the Board's hobbled posture in the mid-1910s. After refusing to get involved for fear of controversy, it was ultimately pulled into the fray because of repeated police interventions that explicitly ignored any jurisdiction the Board of Censorship might claim. A Board ruling condemning the film after two police raids and at least as many appearances before New York magistrates – not to mention after thousands of people had already seen the film – must have been perceived by many as 'too little, too late'.

Still, hoping to solidify its position as the ultimate arbiter of film content in these matters, the Board of Censorship issued a 'Special Bulletin on Social Evil' in February of 1914, carefully delineat-

ing the limited circumstances under which it would permit depictions of the vice trade.[91] Distinguishing between 'indecent pictures' which simply exploited the phenomenon for the purposes of titillation (for which *The Inside of the White Slave Traffic* was a likely model) and 'sex-problem photoplays' which might act as responsible agents of reform (such as *Traffic in Souls*), the Board warned filmmakers that only the latter category would meet its approval. Despite its attempt to exert nationwide influence over film exhibition standards, however, the Board faced competition from many state and municipal censorship bodies which either banned vice films that the Board had passed, or allowed presentations of films it had censured. Even with Board approval, for instance, *Traffic in Souls* was banned in many communities, including New Orleans, Chicago, Montréal, and Pittsburgh.[92] San Francisco, on the other hand, chose to defy the Board's ban on *The Inside of the White Slave Traffic* when an exhibitor there drew 'large throngs' to see the film in late January.[93]

Whether or not the National Board could indeed speak for *national* standards while located in New York also appears to have been of significant concern. Both Fredrick Howe, by then former Chairman of the Board, and Orrin G. Cocks, the Board's newly appointed advisory secretary and a former volunteer committee member who had been involved in the decision regarding *The Inside of the White Slave Traffic*, defended the Board's decision to pass the film in articles published in New York-based reform journals, *The Outlook* and *The Survey*.[94] Evidently fearing that reports of sensational Broadway theatre productions might impugn the Board's standards, Cocks confessed that 'though located in New York ... the National Board does not accept as a basis of criticism the standards of the New York stage or of its complicated liberal and abnormal life'.[95] Instead, Cocks and Howe stressed the contributions made by the city's prominent social organisations to the Board's review committee, insisting that the organisation acted 'on behalf of the general conscience and intelligence of the country' and always sought 'the point of view of typical Americans'.[96] Yet, ultimately its unsatisfactory handling of the white slave films was indicative of the posture that the Board was increasingly forced to adopt in the mid-1910s when its mission became directed more toward fending off proposals for state and federal censorship than exerting national influence over film exhibition.

In the end, the white slave film controversy signalled the arrival of motion pictures as a major cultural force in New York City in 1913: Broadway theatre premières, large crowds, and front-page news coverage. But the question of who would retain control over film exhibition remained open for debate with producers, reformers, police and the Censorship Board all vying for jurisdiction. Most importantly, the controversy located film *content* as the site of struggle, rather than theatrical space, suggesting that the battle was ultimately for the minds of spectators assumed to be profoundly influenced by the films they saw. The tug-of-war over motion picture exhibition certainly did not end when white slave films ceased to occupy centre stage in early 1914, nor were such debates confined to New York City by any means. Rather, the contours of this particular debate staged on the cusp of the classical era allow us to view the forces at work for and against cinema's uplift at this crucial moment.□

Notes

1. *Variety* (19 December 1913), 17.

2. Vice Commission of Chicago, *The Social Evil in Chicago* (Chicago: Gunthorp-Warren, 1911).

3. For more detailed analyses of the white slave films themselves see the following: Robert C. Allen, 'Traffic in Souls', *Sight and Sound* 44, no. 1 (Winter 1974–75): 50–2; Kay Sloan, *The Loud Silents: Origins of the Social Problem Film* (Urbana and Chicago: University of Illinois Press, 1988), 80–6; Kevin Brownlow, *Behind the Mask of Innocence. Sex, Violence, Prejudice, Crime: Films of Social Conscience in the Silent Era* (New York: Alfred Knopf, 1990), 70–85; Shelley Stamp Lindsey, 'Wages and Sin: Traffic in Souls and the White Slavery Scare', *Persistence of Vision* 9 (1991): 90–102; Ben Brewster, 'Traffic in Souls', *Cinema Journal* 31, no. 1 (Fall 1991): 37–56; Richard Maltby, 'The Social Evil, the Moral Order, and the Melodramatic Imagination, 1890–1915', in *Melodrama: Stage, Picture, Screen*, eds., Jacky Bratton, Jim Cook and Christine Gledhill (London: British Film Institute, 1994), 214–30; Janet Staiger, *Bad Women: Representing Female Sexuality in Early American Cinema* (Minneapolis: University of Minnesota Press, 1995), 116–46; and Lee Grieveson,

'Policing the Cinema: *Traffic in Souls* at Ellis Island', *Screen* 38, no. 2 (1997): 149–71.

4. *New York Times* (25 November 1913): 11.

5. *Moving Picture World* (6 December 1913): 1135. Information about seating capacity at Weber's was found in Michael M. Davis, *The Exploitation of Pleasure. A Study of Commercial Recreation in New York City* (New York: Russell Sage Foundation, 1911), 26. Seating capacity for the Park is provided in *New York World* (22 December 1913): 3.

6. *New York Times* (9 December 1913): 8.

7. *New York Tribune* (21 December 1913), section III, 8; and *New York Dramatic Mirror* (24 December 1913): 29.

8. *Variety* (19 December 1913): 17.

9. *Variety* (19 December 1913): 17; and *New York Clipper*, (20 December 1913): 15.

10. *New York Clipper* (13 December 1913): 10.

11. *Variety* (9 January 1914): 12.

12. *Variety* (2 January 1914): 14. *Variety* also suggests that *The Exposure of the White Slave Traffic* might have been a 'general model' for *Traffic in Souls*, since a climatic rooftop raid appears in the earlier film as well as its later, better-known counterpart.

13. *Variety* (9 January 1914): 12.

14. *Variety* (19 December 1913): 16, 17; *New York Dramatic Mirror* (7 January 1914): 38; and Mark Thomas Connelly, *The Response to Prostitution in the Progressive Era* (Chapel Hill: University of North Carolina Press, 1980), 115. The original novel was Reginald Wright Kauffman, *The House of Bondage* (New York: Grosset and Dunlap, 1910).

15. *Variety* (23 January 1914): 14, 24; and *Variety* (20 February 1914): 23.

16. *Motion Picture News* (21 February 1914): 36. See ads in *Moving Picture World* (7 February 1914): 717; *Motion Picture News* (7 February 1914): 10; *Moving Picture World* (14 February 1914): 881; and *Motion Picture News* (14 February 1914): 5. A number of other white slave titles are mentioned in the trade press in late 1913 and early 1914, but I could find no record of when and where they might have played New York. These include: *A Soul in Peril*, *The Shadows of Sin*, which was banned in Kansas City, *The Traffic in Girls* and *The Wages of Sin*, both banned in Pittsburgh. See *Variety* (19 December 1913): 16; *Variety* (30 January 1914), 25; *Variety* (20 February 1914): 25; and *Variety* (27 February 1914): 22.

17. *Moving Picture World* (7 February 1914): 653. Several more white slave pictures continued to be released into the late 1910s, including screen adaptations of stageplays *The Lure* (1914) and *The Fight* (1915), along with *Is Any Girl Safe?* (1916), *The Big Sister* (1916), *It May Be Your Daughter* (1916), *The Little Girl Next Door* (1916) and *Little Lost Sister* (1917).

18. *New York Sun* (29 December 1913): 9.

19. George Kibbe Turner, 'The Daughters of the Poor', *McClure's* 34 (November 1909): 45. Turner's piece followed similar revelations about Chicago's vice district he had penned for the magazine two years earlier: Turner, 'The City of Chicago, A Study of the Great Immoralities', *McClure's* 28 (April 1907): 575–92. The Committee of Fifteen, organised by New York's Chamber of Commerce, had investigated alleged connections between red-light districts and police graft in 1900. The Committee's 1902 report, *The Social Evil*, prefigured vice commission reports issued by many American municipalities in the early 1910s. See, Committee of Fifteen, *The Social Evil*, with special reference to conditions existing in the city of New York, 2nd edn. (New York and London: G.P. Putnam's Sons, 1912).

20. *New York Times* (9 December 1909): 10; and *New York Times* (30 April 1910): 1.

21. 'Five "White Slave" Trade Investigations'. *McClure's* 35 (July 1910): 346; and 'The Rockefeller Grand Jury Report. Showing the Conditions of the 'White Slave Trade in New York City', *McClure's* 35 (August 1910): 471–73. The complete report is reproduced in O. Edward Janney, *The White Slave Traffic in America* (New York: National Vigilance Committee, 1912), 56–75.

22. George J. Kneeland, *Commercialised Prostitution in New York City*, rev. edn. (New York: The Century Co., 1917), 86; and 'Man's Commerce in Women. Mr Rockefeller's Bureau of Social Hygiene Issues Its First Report', *McClure's* 41 (August 1913): 185–89.

23. *New York Dramatic Mirror* 20 (August 1913): 6; *Theatre* (September 1913): xi; *Theatre* (October 1913): 112; and *New York Dramatic Mirror* (10 September 1913): 6, 8. Terry Ramsaye reports that George Loane Tucker, director and co-writer of *Traffic in Souls*, saw *The Lure* and other white slave plays on Broadway that autumn, although Jack Lodge speculates that *Traffic in Souls* was filmed in May of 1913, several months prior to the stage premières. See Ramsaye, *A Million and One Nights* (New York: Simon and Schuster, 1926), 613; and Lodge, 'First of the Immortals: The Career of George Loane Tucker', *Griffithiana* 37 (1989): 41. Film versions of the three best-known stage productions

were subsequently released: *The House of Bondage* premièred in January 1914, while the stage production continued its run. Feature-length film adaptations of both *The Lure* and *The Fight*, including players from the original stage casts, were released in August 1914 and January 1915, respectively.

24. Quoted in *New York Dramatic Mirror* (10 September 1913): 8.

25. 'Muensterberg Vigorously Denounces Red Light Drama', *New York Times* (14 September 1913): 4.

26. 'Dramatizing Vice', *Literary Digest* 47 (1913): 577, 578; *New York Dramatic Mirror* (10 September 1913): 10; and *New York Dramatic Mirror* (17 September 1913): 7.

27. *New York Herald* (10 December 1913): 3.

28. *Moving Picture World* (25 October 1913). Quoted in Kathleen Karr, 'The Long Square-Up: Exploitation Trends in the Silent Films', *Journal of Popular Film* 3, no. 2 (1974): 111.

29. *New York Dramatic Mirror* (17 September 1913): 8.

30. *New York Dramatic Mirror* (20 August 1913): 6.

31. *Moving Picture World* (6 December 1913): 1135; and *New York World* (15 March 1914): M2. See also *New York Times* (3 November 1913): 9.

32. *Variety* (19 December 1913): 17; *New York World* (17 January 1914): 14; *New York Dramatic Mirror* (21 January 1914): 26; and *Variety* (23 January 1914): 14. The *Dramatic Mirror* hinted that Hammerstein might also have been suffering financially as a result of the theatre's conversion, since his commission on box office receipts from 25-cent movie admissions could be considerably less than that generated by stage prices upwards of $2.50 a seat, even taking the film's popularity into account.

33. *New York World* (15 March 1914): M2.

34. On advertising practices during this period see, Leslie Midkiff DeBauche, 'Advertising and the Movies, 1908–1915,' *Film Reader* 6 (1985): 115–24; and Janet Staiger, 'Announcing Wares, Winning Patrons, Voicing Ideals: Thinking About the History and Theory of Film Advertising,' *Cinema Journal* 29, no. 3 (1990): 7.

35. *New York Tribune* (7 December 1913): section III, 8.

36. *New York Tribune* (14 December 1913): section III, 8.

37. *New York Tribune* (22 February 1914): section III, 8.

38. *New York Tribune* (21 December 1913): section III, 8.

39. *New York Tribune* (21 December 1913): section III, 8.

40. *New York Tribune* (22 February 1914): section III, 8.

41. *New York Tribune* (7 December 1913): section III, 8.

42. *Variety* (12 December 1913): 12.

43. *Ibid.*

44. *New York World* (17 December 1913): 11; *Variety* (19 December 1913): 16, 17; and *New York Tribune* (22 December 1913): 4. The *World* later reported that Justice Ten Eyck had requested the elimination of some material from the film and that cuts were subsequently made. It is the only source to report that information. The cuts referred to were likely those made at the request of the National Board of Censorship. See *New York World* (22 December 1913): 3.

45. Quoted in the *New York Dramatic Mirror* (24 December 1913): 28.

46. *New York Sun* (20 December 1913): 1; and *New York Clipper* (27 December 1913): 14.

47. *New York Sun* (21 December 1913): 1; *New York World* (21 December 1913): 1,2; and *New York Clipper* (27 December 1913): 14.

48. *New York Tribune* (22 December 1913): 1, 4; and *New York World* (22 December 1913): 3.

49. *New York World* (22 December 1913): 3; *New York Herald* (22 December 1913): 5; and *New York Tribune* (22 December 1913): 4.

50. *New York Tribune* (24 December 1913): 1; *New York World* (24 December 1913): 3; *New York Herald* (24 December 1913): 4; and *New York World* (25 December 1913): 5.

51. *New York Herald* (23 December 1913): 11; *New York World* (23 December 1913): 3; and *New York Clipper* (27 December 1913): 14.

52. *Variety* (2 January 1914): 14.

53. *New York Tribune* (28 December 1913): 10; *New York World* (30 December 1913): 16; *New York Clipper* (3 January 1914): 14; and *Moving Picture World* (10 January 1914): 156.

54. Quoted in *Variety* (13 March 1914): 23. For coverage of the trial see, *New York World* (17 January 1914): 14; *Variety* (23 January 1914): 15; *Moving Picture World* (31 January 1914): 530; *New York*

World (4 March 1914): 1; *New York World* (5 March 1914): 7; *New York World* (6 March 1914): 9; *New York Dramatic Mirror* (11 March 1914): 31; and *Variety* (13 March 1914): 23. Other employees of the Park and Bijou originally arrested were not indicted.

55. Martin F. Norden, 'New York Mayor William J. Gaynor and His City's Film Industry', *Film Reader* 6 (1985): 79–91; Nancy J. Rosenbloom, 'Between Reform and Regulation: The Struggle Over Film Censorship in Progressive America, 1909–22', *Film History* 1, no. 4 (1987): 314–17; Daniel Czitrom, 'The Politics of Performance: From Theater Licensing to Movie Censorship in Turn-of-the-Century New York', *American Quarterly* 44, no. 4 (1992): 544–48; and Staiger, *Bad Women*, Ch. 4. For information on earlier nickelodeon-era struggles, see Robert A. Armour, 'The Effects of Censorship Pressure on the New York Nickelodeon Market, 1907–09,' *Film History* 4, no. 2 (1990): 113–21; and William Uricchio and Roberta E. Pearson, *Reframing Culture: The Case of the Vitagraph Quality Films* (Princeton: Princeton University Press, 1993), 24–33. It had in fact been Gaynor, then serving as state supreme court justice, who issued the injunction against McClellan's notorious Christmas Eve theatre closings in 1908. Gaynor died in September 1913, and thus did not live to participate in the debate surrounding the white slave films.

56. *Variety* (27 February 1914): 23.

57. *Variety* (12 December 1913): 12; *Moving Picture World* (11 October 1913): 133; and *New York Dramatic Mirror* (24 December 1913): 28.

58. *Variety* (19 December 1913): 17.

59. Quoted in the *New York Dramatic Mirror* (14 January 1914): 57.

60. *Moving Picture World* (7 February 1914): 653. Particularly notable in this regard was the ongoing case between Mutual and the state of Ohio, which had created a censorship body in the spring of 1913. Mutual pursued its case all the way to the Supreme Court which issued a landmark 1915 ruling upholding the rights of states to censor motion pictures, a decision which was not reversed until the 1952 ruling guaranteeing films protection under the First Amendment. See Garth S. Jowett, '"A Capacity for Evil": The 1915 Supreme Court Mutual Decision', *Historical Journal of Film, Radio and Television* 9, no. 1 (1989): 59–78; and John Wertheimer, 'Mutual Film Reviewed: The Movies, Censorship, and Free Speech in Progressive America', *American Journal of Legal History* 37, no. 2 (1993): 158–89.

61. *Moving Picture World* (17 January 1914): 276. On Bush's anti-censorship philosophy, see Richard L.

Stromgren in 'The *Moving Picture World* of W. Stephen Bush', *Film History* 2, no. 1 (1988): 19–20.

62. *New York Dramatic Mirror* (24 December 1913): 28. Also see *New York Dramatic Mirror* (19 November 1913): 28.

63. *Moving Picture World* (11 October 1913): 133; and *Moving Picture World* (17 January 1914): 265.

64. *Variety* (19 December 1913): 17.

65. *Variety* (12 December 1913): 25.

66. *Motion Picture News* (28 February 1914): 58–9.

67. *Variety* (2 January 1914): 14; and *New York World* (23 December 1913): 3.

68. *Moving Picture World* (10 January 1914): 155.

69. *New York Herald* (22 December 1913): 5.

70. *New York World* (25 December 1913): 5.

71. *New York Dramatic Mirror* (17 December 1913): 30; and *New York Clipper* (20 December 1913): 15.

72. 'The White Slave Films', *The Outlook* 106 (17 January 1914): 121; and 'The White Slave Films: A Review', *The Outlook* 106 (14 February 1914): 347–48.

73. Shelley Stamp Lindsey, 'Is Any Girl Safe? Female Spectators at the White Slave Films', *Screen* 37, no. 1 (1996): 1–15.

74. *New York Herald* (22 December 1913): 5; and *New York World* (22 December 1913): 3.

75. From a summary of a *New York Times* editorial presented in *Motion Picture News* (15 November 1913). Quoted in Karr, 117.

76. *New York Tribune* (22 December 1913): 1, 4; *New York World* (29 December 1913): 3; and *New York Tribune* (19 January 1914): 9.

77. *New York World* (24 December 1913): 3.

78. *New York World* (29 December 1913): 3; and *New York Sun* (29 December 1913): 9.

79. *New York Sun* (21 December 1913): 1; and *New York Dramatic Mirror* (31 December 1913): 23.

80. *New York Dramatic Mirror* (31 December 1913): 23.

81. On the formation of the National Board of Censorship see Robert Fisher, 'Film Censorship and Progressive Reform: The National Board of Censorship of Motion Pictures, 1909–22', *Journal of Popular Film and Television* 4, no. 2 (1975): 143–56; Daniel Czitrom, 'The Redemption of Leisure: The National Board of Censorship and the Rise of Motion Pictures in New York City, 1900–20', *Studies in Visual Communication* 10, no. 4 (1984): 2–6; and Rosenbloom, 307–25.

82. A statement released by John Collier, the Board of Censorship's General Secretary, is reprinted in *Motography* (15 November 1913): 339–40.

83. Box 107, Controversial Films Correspondence, National Board of Review of Motion Pictures Collection, Rare Books and Manuscripts Division, New York Public Library (hereafter, NBRMPC).

84. *Ibid.*

85. *Motography* (15 November 1913): 339; and quoted in Fisher, 147.

86. *Moving Picture World* (22 November 1913): 849.

87. *Motion Picture News* (22 November 1913): 34.

88. *Motography* (29 November 1913): 397–398.

89. *Motography* (15 November 1913): 339.

90. Box 105, Controversial Films Correspondence, NBRMPC.

91. Box 171, Subjects Papers, NBRMPC.

92. *Moving Picture World* (3 January 1914): 53; *Variety* (6 February 1914): 22; *Variety* (13 February 1914): 23; *Variety* (20 February 1914): 25; *Variety* (27 February 1914): 22; and Kathleen D. McCarthy, 'Nickel Vice and Virtue: Movie Censorship in Chicago, 1907–15', *Journal of Popular Film* 5, no. 1 (1976): 45.

93. *Variety* (30 January 1914): 24.

94. Frederic C. Howe, 'What To Do with the Motion-Picture Show: Shall It Be Censored?', *The Outlook* 107 (20 June 1914): 412; and Orrin G. Cocks, 'Applying Standards to Motion Picture Films', *The Survey* 32 (27 June 1914): 338. See also John Collier, 'Censorship and the National Board', *The Survey* 35 (2 October 1915): 9–14. Francis G. Couvares provides an excellent overview of the Board's decisions on controversial subjects, including white slavery, in 'The Good Censor: Race, Sex, and Censorship in the Early Cinema', *Yale Journal of Criticism* 7, no. 2 (1994): 233–251.

95. Cocks, 338.

96. Howe, 415; and Cocks, 338.

Film History, Volume 9, pp. 365–376, 1997. Copyright © John Libbey & Company
ISSN: 0892-2160. Printed in Australia

Norimasa Kaeriyama and The Glory of Life

Joanne Bernardi

S tudies of Japanese cinema of the 1910s begin with a now familiar qualification: except for a scant amount of mostly fragments and reconstructions, the actual films made during this period are believed lost. Today the people who worked on these films and the studios where they made them are identifiable by name only. Other than in the pictures in print materials, whole genres exist solely in our imagination, coloured by what we read about them, contemporary with the time or otherwise. Because of this, Japanese cinema of the 1910s is more than anything else a cinema defined by loss. This introduction to and translation of Norimasa Kaeriyama's scenario for his experimental production, *Sei no kagayaki* (The Glory of Life/The Glow of Life, 1919)[1], is part of a study in progress of early screenwriting in Japan. Nearly all that remains of the 'pure film' (*jun'eigageki*) genre of the 1910s, this scenario and, in a broader sense, this lost film, raise questions about our conception of this elusive decade. Given the ambiguous contexture of this period, I offer only a starting point for a consideration of *The Glory of Life* that I hope will be revisited as new materials surface for our consideration.

The question of 'pure film'

The Glory of Life has a poignantly privileged place in the traditional histories of Japanese cinema. Jun'ichiro Tanaka describes it as a beacon of hope, a 'brilliantly shining beam of white light' piercing through what he evidently perceived to be a gloomy future for the Japanese film.[2] Its release was delayed for a year after its completion, which might account

for some of the sensation when it opened. In addition, Kaeriyama, its director, had established a reputation as a frequent contributor to film magazines and was known as a major proponent of 'pure film', a term prevalent in the 1910s in discourse engendered by efforts to reform the industry. Kaeriyama was also a founding editor of *Kinema Record* (originally *Film Record*, 1913), Japan's self-proclaimed (in English) 'illustrated leading cinema trade journal', and the author of *Katsudo shashingeki no sosaku to satsuei ho* (The Production and Photography of Moving Picture Drama, 1917), the only technical handbook of its kind at the time. Because *The Glory of Life* was by no means an unqualified success, it is tempting to argue that Kaeriyama's reputation or, more specifically, that of his theoretical platform, was the single major factor behind the critical attention it received both when it was made, and ever since. Its celebrity exceeds that of Kaeriyama's subsequent works, reputedly better made and more favourably received. Perhaps these films have faded into the background because nothing of them, other than one other unpublished scenario, remains. The scenario for *The Glory of Life* has been published at least three times, and is the first work encountered in the six-volume collection

Joanne Bernardi is assistant professor of Japanese and film at the University of Rochester. Correspondence c/o Modern Languages and Cultures, 409 Lattimore Hall, University of Rochester, Rochester, NY 14627, USA.

of Japanese screenplays edited by the Japanese Association of Screenwriters.[3] When it was first published in an addendum to an 'epoch-making' multivolume screenplay collection commemorating the 40th year of *Kinema junpo* (heir apparent to *Kinema Record*, which folded when Kaeriyama ventured into film production), its inclusion, along with that of *Rojo no reikon* (Souls on the Road, 1921) was likened to 'gilding the lily'.[4]

This kind of hyperbole is put into perspective by a recognition of the loyalties of historians like Tanaka who supported the concept of 'pure film'. As Kaeriyama's debut film, *The Glory of Life*'s position in the trajectory of these histories became that of the first 'pure film' and, by implication, the first indication – that beacon of white light shining in the darkness – that the Japanese film had finally come into its own. When *The Glory of Life* and Kaeriyama's second film, *Miyama no otome* (The Girl in the Mountain/Maid of the Deep Mountains, 1919) were released on the same day, reviews and comments were enthusiastic about Kaeriyama's attempt to try something new, but expressed disappointment in the films themselves. Some commented that his efforts were premature, but at least admitted the films were an indication of hope for the future. The actors were praised for their good intentions, but their acting itself was criticised as 'bland', laughable, or even 'more Western than Japanese'. Kaeriyama was criticised for not being more daring, and more than one viewer felt 'betrayed'.[5] To some extent, it was as if Kaeriyama was being taken to task for making what were merely *shimpageki* (Shimpa films, the prototype for the contemporary drama film) with Western titles. The director Kajiro Yamamoto, enrolled in preparatory courses at Keio University when the films were released, later wrote of his experience seeing the first run of *The Glory of Life*:

> One spring afternoon, after skipping my last class as usual, I took my habitual stroll through the Ginza ... I thought about having a cup of coffee at the Café Paulista and was leisurely walking down Mita slope when I saw a young man passing out handbills. They were made of cheap pink paper (probably the very worst kind) about the size of a postcard, but the printed message caught my eye: 'The first film

[*eiga*] made in Japan'! This catch-phrase announced the opening of *The Glory of Life*, the first production of the Film Art Association and [the director and actors] were all active in the vanguard of the Shingeki theatre movement ... Ah, film! Just seeing that word made my heart race. A film had been made in Japan for the first time. Although there had been moving pictures [*katsudo shashin*] of Shimpa melodramas and Ninjutsu [trick] pictures, there were as yet no films. But now, Japan had given birth to the long-awaited 'film' that was just like that of America ...

> I immediately headed for the theatre. This film, the greatest epoch-making event in the history of Japanese cinema, was opening in a small moving picture hall (movie theatre) called the Toyotama-kan ... About 200 people could fit in the narrow seats, but less than ten percent of the spaces were taken by patrons scattered here and there.

> It was the first Japanese film I had ever seen! Japanese titles of a modern design ... close-ups and moving camera work, the actors' faces untouched by elaborate stage makeup, the plain, unaffected presence of a real woman [female flesh], and the slightly awkward yet straightforward and sincere acting. This was a genuine film. I cried like a baby in the darkness.

> Yet somehow something was missing. The film was rooted in literature, and the acting lapsed into mannerisms from the stage. A true film would not be so crude. Surely film has a more pure, invulnerable, isolated beauty. I was impressed, but at the same time I burned with frustration and anger.[6]

There is some question whether Yamamoto's recollections actually were of *The Glory of Life* or *The Girl in the Mountain*, but his comments are interesting in that they correspond, point by point, to most written accounts of these first two 'pure films' in both contemporary reviews and even more recent references: these were 'films', not just 'moving pictures' (the words *eigageki* and *katsudo shashingeki* were both used throughout the 1910s), with intertitles, cinematic frame composition and editing, naturalistic (verisimilar) acting, and a woman actor instead of a female impersonator (*oyama*), the standard 'female' presence in the industry until the early 1920s. These were in fact the prerequisites of a 'pure film', a concept that in general defined film as a unique, artistically respectable medium independent of certain practices associated with theatre entertainment. These included practices present at both the levels of exhibition and production: benshi accompaniment, stage sets and proscenium framing, heavily coded histrionics, and the prevalence of female impersonators. I say 'in general' because it is entirely unclear to me that this term was universally applied and understood. Although the term was prevalent enough throughout the decade to generate the expression 'pure film movement' (*jun'eigageki undo*), that this 'movement' existed exclusively on a discursive level (at least until the production of Kaeriyama's films) prevented it from becoming formally organised or well defined. However, the starting point for all discussion of 'pure film' was that it was something other than the mainstream commercial Shimpa film or period film (*kyugeki*). In fact, there seems to have been a much wider consensus of what *wasn't* 'pure' than what *was*.[7] An evaluation of *The Glory of Life* as a 'pure film' then is complicated by the absence of a complete understanding of an 'impure' (by connotation) film to which we can compare it.[8]

Aspects of 'pure film'

A detailed analysis of the discussion of 'pure film' prior to the production of *The Glory of Life* is not within the scope of this introduction, and has been addressed elsewhere.[9] It is helpful, however, to acknowledge, if even briefly, some of the factors complicating the definition of 'pure film' during the 1910s. Three aspects of the film world during this period are particularly pertinent to a consideration of *The Glory of Life*: the inherent geographical (Tokyo and Kyoto areas) and genre (contemporary drama film and period film) divisions that continue to characterise the Japanese film world; the symbiotic relationship between formulations of a contemporary drama genre in film (in the 1910s, still classified as 'Shimpa film') and developments in the Shingeki (New Theatre) movement; and the influence of non-Japanese (here, specifically Euro-

Fig. 1. Norimasa Kaeriyama, director of *The Glory of Life*.

American) films, film print materials, and film practice.

Although above I have used the term 'Japanese film industry', our understanding of this industry during the 1910s is compromised by a relative lack of surviving documentation, and incomplete – if colourful – histories. It is well known that from its earliest period Japanese cinema retained the genre distinctions (contemporary and period drama) that characterise the Japanese theatre. This split between two genres has broad implications, because it also encompassed distinctions of place and practice. In other words, it is possible to postulate that there were perhaps different 'industries', loosely divided along generic and geographic lines: historical Kyoto and its environs was favoured for period films, and in general the Tokyo area became the bastion of the Shimpa film after that genre's inception. This was a transitional period marked by changing technology and a trend toward longer films, and subsequent shifts in genre definitions and cinematic practices were even further complicated by regional differences in these definitions and practices as well.[10]

Developments in the two genres were not always parallel. To an extent, 'reform' within each genre depended on the nature of the parent theatrical form. In the case of the contemporary drama genre, the Shimpa melodrama was still popular in the 1910s, but like any form of popular entertainment, it was not immune to senectitude. The concept of a truly 'contemporary' (even modern) contemporary drama film was a key idea in the 'pure film' debate. It was not required that a 'pure film' be a contemporary drama (Kaeriyama's third production, a period film made in Kyoto, is a case in point), but it is important to keep in mind the particular situation Kaeriyama was faced with in situating *The Glory of Life*.

On stage, the contemporary drama could not always accommodate the rapid cultural reconfiguration that took place in Japan after national seclusion ended in the nineteenth century. Kabuki has always been a major form of entertainment, but it stopped being contemporary late in the decade. In some ways Shimpa theatre complemented Meiji (1868–1911) culture with its populist appeal and eclectic mix of Western and Japanese elements. In 1910, shortly after the repertory (now predominantly domestic melodrama) was established within the film industry, it was still popular but on the verge of the same fate as Kabuki.[11] Throughout the 1910s, the borders between the film world and the Shingeki movement, Japan's response to Ibsen and his contemporaries' realist reforms in Europe, blurred as Shingeki writers and actors (among them, Minoru Murata and the other actors Kaeriyama engaged for *The Glory of Life*) moved into film production. Shingeki contributed another important ingredient to *The Glory of Life*: a woman actor (in this case, the Shingeki-trained Harumi Hanayagi) in place of a female impersonator.

But Shingeki did not solve the problem of contemporary representation. Instead it raised new problems by bringing an unprecedented rhetoric to dramatic discourse, as well as the new dimension of a concern for intellectual respectability. Although the Shingeki repertory began with original plays influenced by European drama, its success was based on translations of plays by the likes of Shakespeare, Ibsen, Tolstoy, Chekhov and Gorki. Drama was elevated to literature, and imitation to an art. 'Observe to learn' became a password to culture throughout the decade. For the intellectuals behind the Shingeki movement, the indigenous con-

temporary stage drama fell out of date. As Thomas Rimer notes in his study of Kunio Kishida, a major figure in the movement:

> In a lecture in 1909 on Ibsen's contribution to the world theatre, Shoyo [Tsubouchi] lamented the fact that, although the Japanese had been able to create successful novels in the international style, the low level of the contemporary Japanese theatre represented the greatest shortcoming in all the Japanese arts. Japan, Shoyo insisted, lagged forty years behind the west and had not even been able to imitate, let alone create, western-style drama. Ibsen had led the modernization of the European stage and Ibsen must therefore be studied.[12]

As evident in Kajiro Yamamoto's recollections of Kaeriyama's debut, the entire theoretical debate on 'pure film' was intricately tied to both discussions and observations of film and film practice in the United States and Europe, and a familiarity with imported print materials. This too was part of a larger trend in Japanese culture during the 1910s. As Edward Seidensticker has remarked, this was a period when 'popular entertainments went resolutely international'.[13] *The Glory of Life* and *The Girl in the Mountain* opened on 13 September 1919, and issues of the English language *The Japan Times and Mail* that summer reveal a culture cosmopolitan enough to entertain the average émigré. There are the expected headlines with news of the demobilisation of Europe, and those that suggest a relatively eventful summer on the domestic front ('Hailstorm Spoils Osaka Festival', 'Whale Meat Will be Sold Cheaper than Beef at Public Market'). But in addition there are several announcements of visits to Japan by foreign entertainers ('Russian Operatic Stars Coming to the Imperial'), and advertisements for the upscale Odeon Theatre in Yokohama feature Italian dramas, Christie Brothers comedies, a generous amount of Mabel Normand and *The Triumph of Venus* ('Breezy! Airy! Cool'!).[14]

Another feature of the *Japan Times Weekly and Mail* was a column called 'New Books', a weekly report of recent arrivals at the Maruzen foreign book store in Tokyo. Maruzen was a common source for foreign film magazines and books, including 'how to' manuals like E.W. Sargent's *The Technique of the Photoplay*, which is listed in the bibliography of Kaeriyama's *The Production and Photography of Motion Picture Drama*. Lists of books and magazines from Europe and the United States were also featured in *Kinema Record*. Articles from these publications were sometimes translated and published in Japanese; Kaeriyama's English was good (he wrote some of his articles in *Kinema Record* in English), and much of his first book is heavily indebted to his sources.

Going abroad to tour foreign production sites was also common, beginning at least as early as Ken'ichi Kawaura's trip to the United States before he built a glass stage at the Yoshizawa studio in 1908. This practice culminated at the end of the decade in the 'field trips' taken before the establishment of studios like Kokkatsu and Shochiku, which identified with 'pure film' rhetoric (a third studio, Taikatsu, was established with the help of Thomas Kurihara after he left an acting career behind in Hollywood).[15] Such trips abroad for 'research' were not exclusive to members of the film world, although it is interesting to note that other art practices (theatre, painting) tended to steer toward Europe.

Domestic film magazines featured articles on film industries in both Europe and the United States; as the market for Hollywood films expanded after the mid-1910s, articles describing production methods in Hollywood were common. The influence of Hollywood screenwriting practice in particular is visible in articles like 'Katsudogeki no kyakuhon no kakikata' (How to Write a Script for Moving Picture Drama, in the February 1916 issue of *Katsudo no sekai*), which described the characteristics and features of the continuity format.[16] Detailed synopses and even transcriptions of films from Europe and the United States were featured in magazines like *Kinema Record*, *Katsudo no sekai*, and *Katsudo gaho*. Industry professionals have admitted to reading them for more than just pleasure.[17] But attention was also directed to the potentialities of screenwriting with the 1916 Japanese release of *Cabiria* (1914), which was widely and favourably noted by the intelligentsia.[18]

Finally, an interesting mix of nationalist rhetoric and entrepreneurial spirit emerged over the Japanese film's potential and viability as an international product. There were several aspects to this phenomenon. Racial discrimination toward the

Japanese abroad was a factor. Economics was another: the Hollywood market put pressure on the home front, as revealed, for example, in several cartoons published in *Kinema Record* throughout 1917.[19] The interest in export made not only the female impersonator problematic. It also exacerbated 'pure film' impatience with production and exhibition practices favouring the benshi, and subsequently boosted the interest in debating the mechanics of writing for the screen. Criticism of the mainstream 'line play' (*serifugeki*, a commercial script or film made with benshi accompaniment in mind) was directed toward several aspects of the commercial industry: an ignorance of the importance of a continuity script as a blueprint for production; the prevalence of *kuchidate* (on set narration by the director that undermined preproduction preparation); and the authorial weight given to benshi accompaniment, which precluded the use of intertitles.

Smoke and mirrors?

Kaeriyama has been credited with achieving many 'firsts', and *The Glory of Life* is where he is said to have achieved them. No doubt his reputation in terms of stylistic accomplishments was, and perhaps remains, influenced by the knowledge of and interest in film technology evident in the wide range of technical articles he wrote in *Kinema Record* (*The Production and Photography of Moving Picture Drama* brought together many of these articles). An affinity for the hard sciences evidently ran in the family: Kaeriyama's father was a chemistry teacher and his own background was in engineering. It is not likely to have been a coincidence that Kaeriyama first worked for the short-lived Nippon Kinetophone Company and moved from there to the Tennenshoku Katsudo Shashin Kabushiki Kaisha (The Natural Color Kinematograph Co, Ltd), or Tenkatsu, the company that owned the rights to G.A. Smith and Charles Urban's Kinemacolor process. *The Glory of Life* was financed by Tenkatsu while he was employed there.[20] After directing his last film in 1924, Kaeriyama remained involved in promoting amateur filmmaking, and published film manuals directed at the non-professional reader. His fascination with the technology of film is generally

コダスコープB型

人間の性能に
近き機構

その特長

自　動　裝　填
モーターで捲き返へし
速　　　　　　行
重　心　の　低　き　事
コマを合せる話法
ガッチリしてゐる事
輕　量　携　帯　至　便

EASTMAN KODAK CO., *Rochester, N.Y., U.S.A.*

KAÉRIYAMA'S

CINÉ-HANDBOOK

Published by

THE NIPPON AMATEUR CINEMA LEAGUE

· TOKYO ·

Fig. 2. Frontispiece advertisement (for the Kodascope Model B 16 mm projector) and title page of the first edition of *Kaeriyama's Cine-Handbook* (Tokyo: Nippon Amateur Cinema League, 1930), one of Kaeriyama's manuals for amateur filmmakers.

blamed for his short-lived career as an 'artistic' *auteur.*

It is said that Kaeriyama's greatest achievement was in writing Japan's first continuity script with detailed terminology that suggests a stylistic approach unconventional for the time. The extent and nature of stylistic decisions made during the film's production is unclear, although the cameraman, Masaru Omori (who also used the name Masaru Shibata) had the habit of keeping a daily work diary, some of which he has published, and he has said (albeit rather off-handedly) that the film was basically the same as the published version of the scenario.[21] Anecdotal evidence points to few alterations, although this is impossible to substantiate. Omori mainly remembers having to give up the idea of using actual 'yachts' in the opening scene because 'there weren't any'.[22] Because none of Kaeriyama's works survive, what *The Glory of*

Life (or any of his other films) actually looked like is uncertain. As in the case of reviews, the film's absence limits the kind of information the scenario can provide. Publications of collected screenplays in Japan customarily feature the version of a screenplay that can be identified most closely to the 'vision' of the writer as if it were a finished work (a finite text) in and of itself (independent of the film). Many synopses of the film *The Glory of Life* available in reference books, however, seem to correspond to the published version of Kaeriyama's scenario. In his history of Japanese cinema, Jun'ichiro Tanaka's synopsis of the film is quite different from the published version of Kaeriyama's scenario, and his synopsis is accompanied by an excerpt of a version of the script that also appears to be different from the version I have translated here.[23]

In secondary sources, the history of screenwriting in Japan begins in 1908 with the establishment of the Yoshizawa studio's 'planning department' (*koanbu*), but there appear to be just as few extant early scenarios as there are films. An excerpt from Kiyoshi Masumoto's scenario for a Nikkatsu (Muko-jima studio) Shimpa film *Chichi no namida* (A Father's Tears, 1918) has some of the same details for which Kaeriyama's scenario is known: for example, the terms 'close shot' (*outsushi*), and descriptions of frame composition and acting.[24] Masumoto had been one of the original members of the Yoshizawa 'planning department', was involved in the Shingeki movement, and collaborated with the director Eizo Tanaka on the so-called 're-form' films (*kakushin eiga*) that are considered to be the Shimpa film's equivalent to Kaeriyama's 'pure film'. *A Father's Tears* opened the year before *The Glory of Life*, which suggests that some practices in the Shimpa film might have paralleled what was considered innovative in the work of Kaeriyama.

Masumoto's scenario is different from *The Glory of Life* in many respects. The scenes in *A Father's Tears* are much longer (neither scenario reveals the extent to which the individual scenes might have been broken down into shots). As was the custom in the Shimpa film, the titles are short headings (or sub-titles) more closely resembling the chapter titles in a novel. *A Father's Tears* has extensive dialogue, but no dialogue titles, which suggests the loquacity implied by the term '*serifugeki*'. In a brief commentary published together with the excerpt, Jun'ichiro Tanaka describes the excerpt from *A Father's Tears* as being analogous to the benshi's script (*benshi daihon*).

In circumventing benshi accompaniment, intertitles were indispensable to *The Glory of Life*. In *The Production and Photography of Moving Picture Drama* Kaeriyama promoted the use of intertitles, but advised using them sparingly. In language resembling that of many 'how to' books on scenario writing contemporary to the time, he emphasised the importance of thinking in terms of the screen.[25] Kaeriyama's inclusion of dialogue intertitles appears to be a 'genuine' innovation. Compared with the intertitles, or more correctly, the sub-titles that seem to have characterised the commercial Shimpa film, the variety and range of functions identifiable in Kaeriyama's expository titles are of interest.[26] So is their brevity, particularly when compared to some

of the longer, more 'literary' titles of Minoru Murata's *Souls on the Road*, the most important surviving 'pure film'. Although it is not possible to comment with authority on the actual positioning of the intertitles and their relation to adjacent shots, in the scenario they appear to have been placed with a conscious effort to 'dovetail.' The non-informational aspect of the title 'Two fluttering butterflies' suggests a degree of expressivity that, according to certain reviews of other films, seems to have been complemented by Kaeriyama's visual composition.[27] A frame reproduction of the expository title in scene no. 38 included in a review in *Kinema junpo* reveals it to be an art title (the artist is credited in the scenario along with the rest of the cast and crew).[28] Kaeriyama was evidently not successful in having the film open without benshi accompaniment, but given the nature of the intertitles it is understandable that he requested a benshi skilled in accompanying foreign films.

The non-diegetic title in the final scene of the scenario strikes at the heart of what was judged one of Kaeriyama's great failings. He later wrote that his intention at the time was to make something that resembled a foreign film as closely as possible. To do this, he says, he needed to use foreign films as a model in every respect, and began by writing a continuity 'in a foreign manner'. He writes that he included technical terms (he specifically mentions 'close up', 'insert', 'bust', 'full shot,' 'fade in', 'fade out' and 'iris') following examples he found in imported handbooks, and explains his choice of subject matter in the following manner:

> It was a youthful script entitled 'The Glory of Life'. I had high hopes for the plot, but as a technician with a poor appreciation of literature, I wrote something that could be called a scenario in form only. I was trying to express on film the idea that 'life is effort', and it ended up having a crude, scholarly air, but I thought the plot was substantial for breaking the dull monotony of the Shimpa film.[29]

According to Iyokichi Kondo, who played the role of the young chemist Yamashita, Universal's Bluebird films were a major influence on the scenario. The moral message, the trope of 'bucolic haven versus the urban den of iniquity', and the happy ending could be singled out to invoke the kind of

sentimental melodrama that is said to have characterised the Bluebird Photoplays that seem to have
been popular in Japan at the time.[30] Both Kondo
and Omori have indicated that Minoru Murata,
who played opposite Kondo as the young aristocrat
Yanagisawa, had a hand in rewriting the scenario,
and it is interesting to speculate on the degree and
nature of Murata's input. Murata and Kaeriyama
had been classmates as boys. Either by Kaeriyama's own choice, or because of some antagonism toward him on the part of the regular Tenkatsu
production staff (or a mixture of both),[31] Kaeriyama
looked outside the studio when he cast the film, and
Murata was a fairly well-known member of the
Shingeki movement at the time. He had organised
a small acting troupe, the Torosha, that was receiving favourable reviews for its staging of such
Shingeki staples as Wedekind's *Spring's Awakening* and Ibsen's *Ghosts*. The rest of the cast were
primarily Shingeki actors, including Harumi Hanayagi, who played the third member of the somewhat unlikely love triangle, Teruko. The insert shots
of written text are a possible Shingeki touch – they
do enhance the sense of arid bourgeois respectability – but such epistolary flourishes were not
necessarily foreign to the mainstream Shimpa or
period film. The hint of Turgenev, however, is pure
Shingeki.

Kaeriyama wrote about what he knew. The
'glory of life' that he had in mind was none other
than the sparks given off in an experiment with
'radioactive carbonium' and the black smoke rising
from a factory chimney. In 1918 radioactivity was
about twenty years old; Marie Curie had received
her Nobel prize seven years earlier. Around 1912–
16 the term 'carbonium' was used to describe the
mechanism of some chemical reactions. There is a
class of pigments in plants, called anthocyanins,
that were being studied between 1910–20. There
was controversy as to whether they are oxonium or
carbonium salts. But there is no radioactivity associated with these compounds. There is such a thing
as 'radio-carbon', and Kaeriyama may have taken
some literary liberties with the term because
radioactivity and 'carbonium carbon' were being
discussed at the time.

In Jun'ichiro Tanaka's synopsis of the film, possibly based on his recollections, the plot is somewhat
more elaborate than that of the scenario translated

here. Teruko and Yanagisawa have a child, who is
born after Yanagisawa deserts her and marries the
daughter of a wealthy banker in Tokyo. Yamashita
rescues Teruko just as she is about to fling herself off
a seaside cliff. Yamashita tells Teruko that it is only
the weak who give up the will to live. Teruko
becomes his assistant and helps him research radio-
carbonium. The child born between Yanagisawa
and Teruko becomes ill and dies. Five years pass.
In the meantime, Yamashita builds a splendid factory thanks to the success of his experiments.
Yanagisawa returns, but by now Teruko is happily
married to Yamashita. She scorns his life of leisure
and tells him that although she is but a commoner,
she has found the happiness of a full life. Rejected,
Yanagisawa leaves and Teruko and Yamashita
open their upstairs window to the view of smoke
rising from the factory chimney. They rejoice in the
glory of life.[32]

This synopsis has all the earmarks of a Shimpa
melodrama, but the reviews suggest that at least one
aspect was new, and exciting. Comments on Harumi Hanayagi's performance were generous. Debate over the issue of women on screen as opposed
to the female impersonator was another key feature
of 'pure film' debate, as evidenced in numerous
articles in the trade press. A focus on screen ac-
tresses from Europe and the United States was apparent in Japanese film culture throughout the
1910s. These women are visible throughout
Kinema Record – they were on its covers, its frontispiece and, particularly after 1915, they became the
focus of a variety of feature articles as well. This was
true of such subsequent publications as *Kinema no
sekai*, *kinema gaho*, and *Kinema kurabu*. Women
were not completely absent from the screen. They
appeared most often in chain-dramas (*rensageki*),
a specialty of Tenkatsu, but it was a far from gla-
morous way to make a living.[33] The relative lack of
genre variety was another limiting factor, as wit-
nessed by the interesting career of the chain-drama
actress Yaoko Kinoshita. Her attempt to become the
Japanese Grace Cunard was not successful,[34] but
it is an informative example of the shifting par-
ameters of concepts of female beauty and femi-
ninity. The September 1919 issue of *Katsudo
kurabu* was a special issue on 'Beauties' (*bijin*).
Hanayagi Harumi appears at the end of a collection
of bromides that starts off with such stars as Pearl

Fig. 3. Publicity still of Kaoru Osanai and Minoru Murata on the set of *Joyu den* (Story of an Actress), a Shochiku Russo–Japanese co-production. From *Kinema junpo*, 11 November 1920.

White, Norma Talmadge, Theda Bara, Dorothy Phillips, and a scantily dressed Annette Kellermann in *A Daughter of the Gods* (1916).

Anecdotal accounts of the production of *The Glory of Life* are plentiful. Kaeriyama claims to have started with a script reading of the love scene between Murata and Hanayagi, but the two ended it abruptly in a fit of embarrassed laughter. The actual filming, all done on location, began with the scene of the rainstorm. Locations included the Tokyo YMCA in Kanda, Tokyo station, the lobby of the Kinkikan movie theatre, and the Mitsukoshi department store. The scenes in Ginza were shot from an open car. (Ginza was an urban zone on the ascend-ancy, and Mitsukoshi the most popular store.) Additional shooting was done in Hakone, a resort town near Tokyo. Kondo Iyokichi later wrote that in spite of the dialogue written for the actors, there were many instances when they were only moving their lips.[35]

It took one month to shoot all four reels of *The Glory of Life*. Kaeriyama processed the film along with the cameraman, Omori, and they continued to work together on the editing. Reviews suggest the film was both tinted and toned. Kaeriyama wanted his first two films to open in theatres for foreign films in the popular Asakusa entertainment district, but they eventually opened at two of the better theatres located elsewhere in the city. Opposition from the company benshi is reported to have been the cause of the one year delay.[36]

Critics were finally satisfied with Kaeriyama's third release (his fourth production), *The Girl in His Dreams*, calling it the first Japanese film that could compare favourably with the West. By then Kaeriyama and his colleagues had left Tenkatsu, and with the assistance of the former founder and head of Tenkatsu, Kisaburo Kobayashi, they were producing films under the official title of the Film Art Association (*Eiga geijutsu kyokai*, referred to in *Kinema junpo* as 'L'Association des Artistes Cinematographiques') at Kobayashi's new company, Kokkatsu.When Kobayashi's influence in his own company waned, the group moved to Shochiku at the invitation of Oson Taguchi. For a few months they were managed by Shochiku in the hope that they would provide competition for Kaoru Osanai's newly formed Shochiku Cinema Institute, but on the second film Kaeriyama broke the conditions of their contract by refusing to submit his screenplays for approval. The original staff members soon drifted apart (Murata was one of the first to leave, joining Osanai's Institute, where he directed *Souls on the Road* the following year), and the group disbanded in July 1921. Kaeriyama managed to keep the name of the Film Art Association alive for a few more years, supporting himself by making commercial films for soap and toothpaste. His last film was a commercial failure, ending his career as a director in 1924.

The same month that his first two films opened, Kaeriyama published a diatribe against the 'management' of the film industry, claiming that the only way the Japanese film industry would be 'reformed' was if films were made in a new place (new companies) by new people.[37] Within a year this was on the verge of happening with the establishment of Shochiku and Taikatsu.◻

Acknowledgement

I am grateful to Mamoru Makino for permission to reprint illustrations from the facsimile copies of *Kinema junpo* (Tokyo: Yushodo, 1993).

Notes

1. *Sei no kagayaki* has previously been translated as 'The Glow of Life'. 'kagayaki' can be translated as both 'glow' and 'glory'. An article in Kinema junpo refers to the film in English as 'The Glory of Life'. See Anon., 'New Epoch Will Be Made' [in English], *Kinema junpo* (November 1920): 4.

2. Jun'ichiro Tanaka, *Nihon eiga hattatsu shi* (Tokyo: Chuo koronsha, 1975), vol. 1, 282.

3. Takehiko Mizusawa (Norimasa Kaeriyama), 'Sei no kagayaki', *Nihon shinario taikei*, ed. Shinario sakka kyokai (Tokyo: Eijinsha, 1973), vol. 1, 7–17. My translation was made from this most recent publication of the scenario. The first imprint of *The Glow of Life* in 1959 was based on a carbon copy of the scenario that Kaeriyama had kept in his home. He had written it himself on Mino paper, a particularly sturdy type of Japanese paper from Gifu prefecture. See 'Henshu o owatte', in *Nihon eiga daihyo shinario zenshu* (Tokyo: Kinema junpo, 1959), vol. 6, 180. The scenario is on pages 157–161. The scenario has also been published in *Nihon eiga shinario koten zenshu* (Tokyo: Kinema junpo, 1965), vol. 1, 14–21. Except for the addition of a number '2' after the heading for scene no. 21 in this version, all three versions are identical.

4. *Nihon eiga daihyo shinario zenshu* ,vol. 6, 156.

5. See, for example, the following reviews of *The Glory of Life, The Maid in the Mountain* and *Gen'ei no onna* (The Girl in His Dream, 1920): *Kinema junpo* (1 October 1919): 2, 4; (11 October 1919): 7–8; (1 June 1920): 4, 10; (11 June 1920): 4; *Katsudo no sekai* (October 1919), *Katsudo kurabu* (November 1919): 44–45. Selected reviews are also included in *Kaeriyama Norimasa to Tomasu Kurihara no gyoseki*, ed. Okabe Ryu, Nihon eigashi soko no. 8 (Tokyo Film Library Council, 1973), 21–28. *The Glory of Life* and *The Maid in the Mountain* were completed in 1918. Their release was delayed until 13 September 1919, when they opened simultaneously at two different theatres.

6. Kajiro Yamamoto, *Katsudoya suiro* (Tokyo: Chikuma Shobo, 1965), 31–33. Kishi Matsuo believed that Yamamoto confused his recollections of Kaeriyama's first films, and in this passage he is actually referring to the second film, *The Girl in the Mountain* (the theatre Yamamoto refers to is the one in which this film, not *The Glory of Life*, opened. See Kishi Matsuo, *Jinbutsu nihon eiga shi* (Tokyo: Dabiddosha, 1970), 265–66. 'Film Art Association' is my translation of *Eiga geijutsu kyokai*, the name chosen by Kaeriyama's production group. This group is referred to as 'L'Association des Ar-

tistes Cinématographiques' in Anon, 'New Epoch Will Be Made'.

7.   See for example the 'Questions and Answers' column of *Kinema junpo* (11 August 1920): 4. In response to a reader who apparently inquired about why the term 'pure film' (*jun-eiga-geki*) had been applied in a particular case, the writer offers his interpretation of the term as meaning 'that which possesses all the elements of a film drama [*eiga-geki*] and goes beyond being a film adaptation [*eiga-ka*] of a stage play [*butai-geki*]', then suggests that the term was used to market Kaeriyama's *The Girl in His Dream* and Yoshiro Edamasa's *Aware no kyoku* (Song of Sadness, 1919) because they were 'more advanced than other Japanese films until now and closer to Western films'. The writer suggests that the use of the term to advertise a particular film in question was just good marketing.

8.   It is interesting to note that the historiographical tendency is to refer to 'progressive' Shimpa films like those of Eizo Tanaka and Tadashi Oguchi, many of which were written by the Shimpa/Shingeki playwright Kiyoshi Masumoto, as 'reform(ed) films' (*kakushin eiga*), while films that overtly laid claim to being inspired by films of 'the West' are classified as 'pure films'. David Bordwell's analysis of the 1922 Shimpa film *Futari Shizuka* provides a clear picture of the visual style of this ostensibly 'impure' genre only four years after the production of *The Glory of Life*. See Bordwell, 'Visual Style in Japanese Cinema, 1925–1945' in *Film History 7* (1995): 5–31. For an example of a 1910s Kabuki (*kyuha* or *kyugeki*) film, *Goro Masamune* (1915), see Hiroshi Komatsu, 'From Natural Colour to the Pure Motion Picture Drama: The Meaning of Tenkatsu Company in the 1910s of Japanese Film History' in *Film History 7* (1995): 81–86.

9.   I have discussed some of the issues involved in 'The Pure Film Movement and the Contemporary Drama Genre in Japan' in *Film and the First World War*, ed. Karel Dibbets *et al.* (Amsterdam: Amsterdam University Press, 1995): 50–61, and 'Tanizaki Jun'ichiro's 'The Present and Future of the Moving Pictures' in *Currents in Japanese Culture*, ed. Amy Vladeck Heinrich (New York: Columbia University Press, 1996): 291–308. Both articles are based on research I discuss in more detail in *The Early Development of the Gendaigeki Screenplay: Kaeriyama Norimasa, Kurihara Tomas, Tanizaki Jun'ichiro and the Pure Film Movement* (PhD dissertation, Columbia University, 1992). Aspects I focus on in this transitional period are also discussed from a different perspective in Aaron Gerow, *Writing a Pure Cinema: Articulations of Early Japanese Film* (PhD dissertation, University of Iowa, 1996).

10.   I am grateful to Yoneo Ota for our conversations concerning his research on set design in the Japanese film industry. Ota brought my attention to the degree, for example, to which the concept and function of (and terminology for) 'set' and 'set designer' in Kyoto was affected by the extent to which the 'set' for a period film, a major part of Kyoto production, was a location that companies there could customarily take for granted.

11.   See J. Thomas Rimer, *Toward a Modern Japanese Theatre: Kishida Kunio* (New Jersey: Princeton University Press, 1974), 15–16.

12.   *Ibid.*, 19. Bordwell discusses in detail some of the dynamics and implications of this 'cultural exchange' in 'Visual Style in Japanese Cinema', 14–18.

13.   Edward Seidensticker, *High City Low City: Tokyo from Edo to the Earthquake* (New York: Knopf, 1983), 274. Seidensticker emphasises the role film played in putting international celebrities 'in front of everyone'.

14.   *The Japan Times Weekly and Mail*, July–September, 1919.

15.   Kokkatsu, Shochiku, and Taikatsu are the abbreviated names for *Kokusai eiga kabushiki kaisha*, *Shochiku gomei kaisha* and *Taisho katsuei* (originally 'katsudo') *kabushiki kaisha*.

16.   Nakura Bun'ichi, 'Katsudogeki no kyakuhon no kakikata' (February 1916): 70–77.

17.   I discuss this phenomenon in more detail in *The Early Development of the Gendaigeki Screenplay*. One example is Kiyohiko Ushihara, who has written that his scenario for *Souls on the Road* was influenced by transcriptions of films from the United States (Ushihara, forward to the scenario for *Souls on the Road* in *Nihon eiga shinario koten zenshu*, vol. 1, 22). See also Matsuo Kishi, 'Kaisetsu: shinario tanjo izen', in *Nihon shinario taikei*, vol. 1, 797.

18.   A special supplement dedicated to the Japanese opening of *Cabiria*, which was imported by the enterprising Kisaburo Kobayashi, appears in the June 1916 issue of *Katsudo no sekai*. See also the playwright Shiko Tsubouchi's article 'Cabiria inshoki' in the same issue (2–3). The previous issue of *Katsudo no sekai* featured a special section on writing for film, 'Katsudogeki kyakuhon ni tsuite' (On Scripts for Moving Picture Drama), (May 1916): 24–55, which I discuss in detail in *The Early Development of the Gendaigeki Screenplay*, 217–220.

19.   Hollywood's flush economy was an object of considerable comment, and envy. One cartoon in particular lampoons Hollywood's iron grasp on the

international market. *Kinema Record* no. 41 (10 November 1916): 523. See also Anon., 'Kyakuhon o eiga ni suru made', *Katsudo gaho* (September 1917): 76–79. After estimating the itemised cost of an average Hollywood production, the writer observed that it was little wonder the Americans could afford to spend such grand amounts, considering the average number of viewers there in one day totalled '2,900,000 people, or one-fourth the entire population'.

20. See Komatsu, 'From Natural Colour to the Pure Motion Picture Drama', 69–81 for a detailed account of Tenkatsu, including a good picture of what else was being made by the company while Kaeriyama was employed there.

21. Masaru Omori, 'Sosoki no kameraman' in ed. Shohei Imamura et al., *Koza Nihon eiga* (Tokyo: Iwanami shoten, 1985), vol. 1, 229–230.

22. Masaru Shibata (Omori), 'Jun'eigageki to kouta eiga', in ed. Kenji Iwamoto et al., *Kinema no seishun* (Tokyo: Libroport, 1988): 18.

23. I discuss Tanaka's synopsis below. In an article written to commemorate one decade since the production of *The Glory of Life*, Kaeriyama included an excerpt of the scenario that corresponds to the published version translated here. See 'Junen mae no hanashi', *Eiga jidai* vol. 5 no. 4 (October 1928): 109.

24. This excerpt appears in Jun'ichiro Tanaka, 'Onoe Matsunosuke-geki *Bingo Saburo*, Mukojima shimpageki *Chichi no namida*, Yamazaki Naganosuke rensageki *Utashigure*, Sawamura Shirogoro-geki *Joso ninjutsu*', in *Horidasareta meisakusen*, suppl. to *Nihon eiga shinario koten zenshu* (Tokyo: Kinema junpo, 1966), 27–29. I have not been able to locate the original script, presumably part of Tanaka's personal collection, which has been long since dismantled.

25. See Kaeriyama's chapter on the scenario and the scenario writer, *Katsudo shashingeki* 2nd edn. (Tokyo: Seikosha, 1921), 41–88.

26. For a discussion on the functions of expository titles, see Brad Chisholm, 'Reading Intertitles' in *Journal of Popular Film and Television* 15 (Fall 1987): 137–142.

27. A review of *The Girl in the Mountain* describes the poetic effect of silhouette lighting in an exterior scene. Tominosuke Sokyu, 'Senkusha no kage' in

Katsudo kurabu (November 1919): 44. Accounts of the film often mention Kaeriyama's attempt to experiment with new kinds of artificial lighting. For example, see Kaeriyama, 'Junen mae no hanashi', 111.

28. Shunbisei Kyobashi, 'Miyama no otome kokuhyoki', *Kinema junpo* (11 October 1919): 8. Jun'ichiro Tanaka attributes the first use of art titles to Eizo Tanaka.

29. Norimasa Kaeriyama, 'Junen mae no hanashi', 108–110. There is an undeniable hint of dogmatism to Kaeriyama's writing, and the punctuation is atrocious. I'm indebted to my colleague Mariko Tamate for helping me with a few of the murkier spots.

30. Iyokichi Kondo, 'Yukeru eiga geijutsu kyokai', in *Kaeriyama Norimasa to Kurihara Tomasu*, 63. The amount and kind of attention given to the Bluebird films is interesting in that descriptions of the films often reveal a perceived affinity with the Shimpa film. The Bluebird films were also admired for their use of natural locations, which is notable in view of the attention given to the natural landscape in *The Glory of Life*.

31. Omori suggests the regular production crew at Tenkatsu resented the fact that the company seemed to be favouring him over more experienced people like Yoshiro Edamasa. Edamasa's 'pure film', *Song of Sadness*, was made shortly after *The Glory of Life*, but was also held from release for about a year. See Omori, 'Jun'eigageki to kouta eiga', 18–19.

32. Tanaka, *Nihon eiga hattatsu shi*, 284–85.

33. The chain drama actor's day started early, with location shooting, and was long. The actors were virtually 'on call' throughout the duration of the mixed media performance, supplying voices for the filmed parts of the drama.

34. See, for example, Yaoko Kinoshita, 'Rakuba no hanashi' (Falling Off My Horse), in *Katsudo gaho* (April 1917): 68–71.

35. Kondo, 'Yukeru eiga geijutsu kyokai', 38. See Kaeriyama, 'Eiga seisaku no omoide', *Kaeriyama Norimasa to Kurihara Tomasu*, 35, and Chieo Yoshida, *Mo hitotsu no eigashi* (Tokyo: Jiji tsushinsha, 1978), 93–96.

36. Norimasa Kaeriyama, 'Aru hi aru hito no hanashi' in *Katsudo kurabu* (September 1919): 148–151.

Film History, Volume 9, pp. 377–387, 1997. Copyright © John Libbey & Company
ISSN: 0892-2160. Printed in Australia

Appendix: The Glory of Life screenplay translation

Joanne Bernardi

Credits:

Original Story: Takehiko Mizusawa (Nori-masa Kaeriyama)
Director: Norimasa Kaeriyama
Photography: Masaru Omori
Titles: Tatsu Nogawa

Cast:

Yasuhiko Yanagisawa: Minoru Murata
Juntaro Yamashita: Iyokichi Kondo
Teruko Shimazaki: Harumi Hanayagi
Yo-chan: Yoichi Ishida
Teruko's father: Sugisaku Aoyama

1. On the lake

Title: 'SUMMER HAS ARRIVED. HE HAS COME TO THE RESORT, AS HE DOES EVERY YEAR.
The Viscount's son, YASUHIKO YANAGI-SAWA ... MINORU MURATA'
Yasuhiko is sailing his yacht on the lake.
(2–3 shots, add a close-up)

2. Near the lake #1

Title: 'YAMASHITA AND TERUKO HAVE BEEN FRIENDS SINCE CHILDHOOD. The young chemist, JUNTARO YAMASHITA ... IYOKICHI KONDO

The well-to-do young woman, TERUKO SHIMA-ZAKI ... HARUMI HANAYAGI'
Yamashita and Teruko are about to put their boat in the water.

3. Near the lake #2

Title: 'YO-CHAN, Teruko's younger brother ... YOICHI ISHIDA'
Yo-chan comes running toward the lake from afar. As he runs forward, he looks ahead and laughs.
Yo-chan : 'Sister!'
(Close-up) Yo-chan's face. He breaks into a run.

4. Near the lake #1

Yamashita and Teruko push their boat into the water. Yo-chan comes running toward them.
Yo-chan: 'Please take me too.'
Yamashita: 'Oh, it's you – get in.'
Teruko: 'Yo-chan, don't rock the boat, it's dangerous.'
Yo-chan: 'Don't worry, I won't.'
Yamashita and Yo-chan launch the boat. Teruko gets on board. The other two also get in and they take off.

5. On the lake

Yanagisawa's yacht sailing on the lake. The yacht carrying Yamashita and the others sails behind it. The two boats gradually draw nearer to each other until Yamashita and Yanagisawa are sailing neck and neck. They race their yachts.

6. The shore of the lake

The two boats reach the shore. The four passengers disembark and walk ashore. Yamashita introduces Teruko to Yanagisawa.
Yamashita: 'Allow me to introduce you. This is Miss Shimazaki.'
Yanagisawa: 'How do you do. My name is Yanagisawa. My summer house is in the neighbourhood, so please come visit.'
Teruko: 'Why, thank you, I will.'
Yanagisawa is moved by Teruko's beauty.
Yanagisawa: 'Well, let's meet again.'
Yamashita: 'Goodbye, we'll stop by to visit you sometime.'
Yanagisawa says goodbye and leaves. The remaining three watch him depart. Teruko looks thoughtful as she gazes after him.
(Insert setting sun.) Fade out.

7. The garden of Yanagisawa's summer house

Title: 'THE AWAKENING OF LOVE'
In the garden, Yangisawa is gazing at the lake. (It is toward evening, at dusk.) The evening moon illuminates the ground. Yanagisawa recalls the events of the day, and Teruko's face. (Insert: the two yachts, and Teruko's face)

8. At a window, Teruko's house

Outside it is dark, and a chill wind blows in through the window. Teruko sits in a chair by the window, with a lamp beside her. She is slightly slouched in the chair, reading a novel.
(Close-up) Teruko and her book. The title is visible:
'A Nest of Gentlefolk' by Turgenev.
(Back to) Teruko, her book slips from her hands.

Teruko's face is clearly visible – she is lost in thought.
(Close-up) Teruko's face. She looks hesitant.
(Back to) Teruko, reflecting on what happened earlier in the day.
Title: 'IF ONLY IT WOULD COME TRUE ...'
(Vision) Teruko and Yanigisawa riding in an automobile. (Fade out)

9. Yamashita's laboratory

Yamashita works alone on his research.

10. In the woods #1

Title: TWO FLUTTERING BUTTERFLIES (Insert)
Yanagisawa awaits Teruko by some tall trees in the woods.

11. In the woods #2

Teruko, walking on her way to see Yanagisawa.

12. In the woods #3

Yanagisawa seen from a distance. Teruko approaches him, recognises him, and runs toward him.

13. Back to In the woods #1

Yanagisawa and Teruko holding hands as they take a walk together.
Teruko: 'Could you please slow down?'
Yanagisawa: 'No, I had to wait for you quite a long time. I was just beginning to think that you might not come.'
Teruko: 'Really? ... let's take a walk over there.'
The two of them walk off.

14. On the mountain

Yanagisawa and Teruko walking and chatting. Yanagisawa asks,
Title: 'WHAT IS YOUR PHILOSOPHY OF LIFE?'
Fingering some flowers, Teruko answers cheerfully.
Title: 'LIFE? WELL, ONE SHOULD BE HAPPY

AND LIVE A FULL LIFE, OF COURSE … I HATE A GLOOMY OUTLOOK, YOU KNOW.'
As soon as Yanagisawa hears this, he says,
Title: 'YES. WE SHOULD EAT WHATEVER WE WANT AND DO WHATEVER WE LIKE. ONE MUST LIVE LIFE TO THE FULLEST.'

15. On the mountain

16. On the mountain

(same. LS, fade out)

17. Teruko's father's room

Title: 'TERUKO'S FATHER IS AN ARDENT OLD BOTANIST – OBLIVIOUS TO EVERYTHING BUT HIS WORK.
Teruko's father … SUGISAKU AOYAMA.'
Surrounded by numerous old books and plant specimens, Teruko's father is engrossed in studying something under his microscope. Beside him Yo-chan is looking through his father's magnifying glass at insects in a box.
(Close-up) Yo-chan looks at the insects. A shot of the insects fighting.
Yo-chan: 'Come on, come on – no, no good, you lost.'
His father notices his loud voice, looks up from his microscope and scolds Yo-chan.
Father: 'What are you saying? Go away, you're too noisy.'
As if making fun of his father, Yo-chan squints with one eye, makes a face and leaves. His father is in a huff, but quickly turns his attention back to his work.

18. The garden, #1:1 (fade in)

Title: 'ONE MORNING'
Yamashita, Yangisawa, and Teruko are playing tennis.

19. The garden #2:1

Yo-chan and a group of other children are imitating their favourite movie actors.

20. The garden #1:2

Tennis.

21. The garden, and Teruko's father's room #2

The father, engrossed in his research.

22. The garden #2:2

Yo-chan imitates Charlie Chaplin.

23. The garden #1:3

A tennis ball flies through the air. Teruko makes a face as she misses it.

24. Again, Teruko's father's room #2

The ball hits Teruko's father in the face. He is startled, and angry.

25. The garden #1:4

Teruko: 'Let's quit, my father's annoyed.'
Yanagisawa: 'Well then, shall we go?'
Yamashita: 'I'll catch up with you. I'm going to straighten up a bit here before I go.'
Teruko: 'Thank you, I'm sorry to leave this to you.'
They leave, and Yamashita gathers up the rackets, balls and other equipment.

26. In the shade of some trees #1

Teruko arrives first and sits on the grass.
Teruko: 'Why don't you come over here where it's cool.'
Yanagisawa: 'Me? I 'm covered with sweat. It certainly is hot.'
Yanagisawa sits down. Teruko discovers a caterpillar on his sleeve.
Teruko: 'Wait, just a minute –'
Yanagisawa: 'What? There's nothing there. What a nuisance you are!'
Teruko: 'No, see – a caterpillar!'
(Close-up, Teruko grabs the caterpillar).
Yanagisawa: 'What a horrible feeling. I won-

der where it came from.'
Teruko flicks the caterpillar away. Yanagisawa wipes his hands on his clothes.

27. A road at night

Yamashita approaches.

28. In the shade of some trees #2

Yanagisawa gives Teruko a gift. As they happily embrace, Yamashita comes from behind and approaches them warily. Teruko sees him and stands up.
Yamashita: 'Teruko! Why, I didn't realise … is it all right for me to have come?'
Teruko: 'Of course. There's something I forgot to do. I'll be back.'
Yanagisawa: 'Teruko, can't it wait?'
Teruko: 'But I'll be back.'
Yanagisawa: 'Then, I'll be seeing you …'
Yamashita gazes after Teruko as she leaves.

29. The garden 2:3

(Insert, fade in and out) The children playing in the garden.

30. In the shade of some trees #2

Yamashita speaks to Yanagisawa.
Title: 'DO YOU LOVE HER?'
Yanagisawa: 'Well, I don't know. I'm not really sure.'
Yamashita: 'I see.'
He looks uneasy. He tries to hide his growing anger as he continues,
Yamashita: 'But, think about what you're doing.'
Yanagisawa: '– what does it matter?'
Yamashita: 'What do you mean, what does it matter –'
Title: 'THERE IS NO NEED FOR ME TO THINK ABOUT TOMORROW, OR ANYTHING OTHER THAN MY PRESENT HAPPINESS.'
Yamashita: 'I see – then goodbye.'
He leaves, and Yanagisawa looks annoyed at having been caught in the act by Yamashita, of all people.

31. In the shade of some trees in the garden

Teruko looks out from between some trees. Yamashita approaches. Teruko hides. Looking sad, Yamashita walks right by her hiding place. Teruko sticks her head out once again. (Close-up) A Close-up of Teruko, her eyes filled with tears. She leaves her hiding place.

32. Under the shade of some trees #3

Teruko approaches Yanagisawa. Yanagisawa placates her.
Yanagisawa: 'You mustn't worry. What is there to worry about?'
Teruko hides her tear-streaked face. Then the two of them exchange a meaningful look, and passionately embrace one another.
(Close-up) The expression on Teruko's face as it wavers between apprehension and joy.
(Close-up) Yanagisawa's face: there are traces of uneasiness, but his expression also seems to be reassuring Teruko. (Slow fade out)

33. A table by the lakeside

Yasuhiko Yanagisawa, Teruko, and her younger brother are seated around the table, eating a meal. A manservant approaches the garden with a telegram. (Insert Close-up) The telegram:
'FATHER CRITICAL RETURN IMMEDIATELY YANAGISAWA'
Yanagisawa is alarmed. Because he is facing Teruko, he composes himself and tries to hide the telegram. Teruko notices, and looks at him.
Teruko: 'What is it?'
Yanagisawa: 'It's nothing …'
Teruko (reaching for the telegram): 'Something must have happened. Please let me have a look.'
Yanagisawa makes a move to intercept her, but she forcibly snatches it out of his hand and reads it. She stares at him in surprise and concern.
Yanagisawa: 'I must go home.'
Teruko: 'Are you leaving, then? I suppose it can't be helped.'

With a look of resignation, Yanagi-sawa abruptly rises from his chair. Teruko sighs, shaken by this turn of events.

34. A room

Yanagisawa prepares for his trip. His maid and a steward look concerned as they assist him. (Appropriate conversation)

35. In front of Yanagisawa's summer house

An automobile is waiting. Yanagi-sawa and Teruko come out of the house. They stand in front of the automobile. (With servants, attendants)

Yanagisawa: 'I plan to return right away. There's no need for you to be concerned, I'll be sending you a letter directly.'

Teruko: 'Yes, please let me know how things are as soon as you can. I'd like to go with you as far as the railway station ...'

Title: 'I'LL BE BACK SOON, AND WHEN I DO RETURN WE'LL HAVE MUCH TO TALK ABOUT – GOODBYE.'

Teruko: 'Goodbye, please write ...' They exchange glances, and Yanagisawa gets into the automobile. It drives off. Teruko stares after it.

Fig. 1. Frame reproductions of a shot of Harumi Hanayagi as Teruko and art title for expository title, *The Glory of Life*, scene 38. From *Kinema junpo*, 11 October 1919.

36. A road

An automobile travels rapidly along the road. (Fade out)

37. Teruko's father's room #2

Teruko's father and Yamashita are discussing some scientific matter.

Father: 'Yamashita, yesterday I went into the mountains. I made an interesting discovery.'

Yamashita: 'Really? What is it?'

Father: 'Well, take a look in the microscrope. I have never seen anything so magnificent.'

Yamashita takes a look.

(Close-up) Microbes seen through the microscope.

Yamashita: 'Indeed! Where did you discover this?'

Father: 'Isn't it something? On the far mountain, to the back of the range ...'

Teruko enters looking sad. She looks the other way. Her father notices.

Father: 'Teruko, what is the matter? You don't look well at all.'

Teruko: 'It's nothing ...'
Understanding something of the situation, Yamashita sighs. Teruko's father acts as though nothing of concern is going on.
Father: 'I'm going back to the same place again. I'd like to collect some better samples.'
The two men continue their conversation. Teruko walks across the room. (She looks very sad.)

38. Teruko's bedroom (night)

Title: 'DAY AFTER DAY, MONTH AFTER MONTH THE TIME PASSES, BUT NO NEWS ARRIVES FROM YANAGISAWA'
In her white nightgown, Teruko sits at her desk. She is overcome with sadness as she gazes at a photograph of Yanagisawa.
(Close-up) Yanagisawa's photograph.
She extinguishes the lamp and gets into bed. But she has trouble sleeping, and stares at the ceiling with her eyes wide open. Growing increasingly despondent, she bursts into tears.

39. Tokyo

Title: 'YANAGISAWA IS HELD CAPTIVE BY THE SEDUCTIVE DREAM OF CITY LIFE'
Yanagisawa and an actress leave the Teikoku Theater by car. They drive through the streets of Ginza, arriving at the Mitsukoshi Department Store.

40. The laboratory

(Quick Fade in and out) Yamashita's room. He is conducting an experiment.

41. Behind Teruko's house (night)

Teruko quietly opens the back gate and leaves, inching along the wall.

42. In front of the railway station

Teruko enters the railway station.

43. A platform

Teruko boards a train.

44. Inside the train

Title: 'VISITING YANAGISAWA IN TOKYO'

45. Railroad tracks

The train moves off into the distance. (Fade out)

46. In front of Tokyo station

Teruko exits the station.

47. On the road

Walking along the road, Teruko stops to ask a passerby for directions to the house of Viscount Yanagisawa. The person points out the house.

48. The wall of Viscount Yanagisawa's residence

Nodding in recognition, Teruko walks toward the gate.

49. In front of the gate

Teruko hesitates before entering the wide gate.
(Close-up) The hesitant expression on Teruko's face.
After a moment, the sound of a carriage (automobile) is heard.

50. An automobile travelling along the road

The automobile approaches. Yanagisawa and the actress are inside.

51. Back to the gate

Teruko attempts to hide as the automobile enters the gate. Teruko recognises it. She steps out to look through the gate at what is inside.

52. Beside a telephone pole

Teruko looks around, then leans against a telephone pole. Stunned and weak, she bursts into tears. She then leaves. (Fade out)

53. Inside the train

Teruko sadly looks out the train window.
(Fade out)
Title: 'RETURNING HOME AGAIN'

54. A road in Teruko's hometown (night)

Teruko walks home alone through the picturesque natural landscape of mountains and trees.

55. In front of the house

She approaches her house. Pausing for a moment, she enters.

56. Teruko's father's bedroom

Teruko's father is asleep. Teruko quietly opens the door, looks in on him, and then closes the door again.

57. Teruko's bedroom

Teruko listlessly enters her bedroom. After a pause, she collapses onto the bedding and cries. Finally, she undresses.

58. The laboratory (night)

Yamashita reads a book as his assistant yawns beside him. Soon Yamashita also grows tired. He taps his assistant on the shoulder to say that he is going out for a walk and will return.

59. Teruko's bedroom

Teruko lies in bed, but her mind is in a turmoil and she is unable to sleep.

(Vision) The mocking faces of frightful demons, Yanagisawa's face and then Yamashita's stern face come to mind. In a half mad state, she leaves the room (her face strangely composed).

60. Alongside the house (night)

Teruko leaves the house in her bare feet.

61. Lakeside #1 (night)

Teruko runs toward the riverbank. She gets into a boat that is tied up there and pushes off.

62. On the lake (night)

She throws the boat's oars into the water and, sadly, stands up in the boat. Her decision is made.

63. Lakeside #2 (night)

Yamashita is taking a walk when he sees a boat out on the lake. Noticing someone dressed in white, he breaks into a run.

64. Lakeside #3 (night)

Yamashita pushes off in a boat and begins to row.

65. On the lake

Yamashita rows the boat. An empty boat drifts toward him. Looking ahead he sees a woman's body floating in the water and hastens toward it.

66. On the lake

Yamashita lifts the woman out of the water.

67. Aboard the boat

Yamashita, having saved Teruko, rows the boat.

68. The shore of the lake

The boat reaches the shore. Yamashita walks ashore with Teruko in his arms.

69. Within the gate of Teruko's house

Yamashita holds Teruko in his arms. A maid comes out of the house and together she and Yamashita help Teruko inside.

70. Teruko's bedroom

Yamashita brings Teruko into the bedroom. Her father enters in his night clothes. The maid is busily attending to things. Teruko's father tells Yamashita to give Teruko some smelling salts, and the maid helps her out of her wet clothes. Yamashita leaves to go for the doctor.

71. In front of the gate and within the gate

Yamashita hurries to the doctor's by car.

72. An automobile travelling along the road

73. In front of the Doctor's house

Yamashita gets out of the car, bangs on the door and calls out. The doctor comes out.

74. Teruko's bedroom

Teruko has changed her clothes and is asleep in bed. Yamashita and the doctor hurry to her side. The doctor promptly looks at her and says, 'She's all right. There is no need to be concerned'. Everyone is relieved. Teruko moves slightly.

75. Teruko's bedroom (morning)

Title: 'THE MORNING LIGHT'
The window is open, and the morning sun streams into the room. Teruko remembers nothing from the day before and attempts to get out of bed. Her head feels slightly heavy. She forces herself to get up, and she goes to the window to look outside.

76. A part of Teruko's house

Yamashita pays a visit. He meets Teruko's

father in the garden, briefly greets him and hastens to Teruko's room.

77. Teruko's bedroom

Yamashita's entrance takes Teruko completely by surprise. She hurriedly throws some clothes on over her night dress and awkwardly sits on the bed. Yamashita sits down in a chair in front of her.
Yamashita: 'How are you doing? Do you feel better?'
Teruko: 'Yes.'
She answers him, then sadly turns away, her head bowed. Sympathetic as well as reassuring, Yamashita says:
'This won't do, what is it that is making you sad?'
Title: 'LAST NIGHT YOU TRIED TO DIE ...'

78. Talking about the night before (insert)

Title: 'THIS IS THE ULTIMATE DILEMMA. WE MUST WORK FOR LIFE WITH AN EFFORT GREATER THAN DEATH. WE STRIVE. WE WORK. IT IS THE COWARD WHO BECOMES FRUSTRATED IN THE ENDEAVOR TO LIVE AND HASTENS DEATH ...'
Teruko gradually takes heart.

79. The interior of the church

The children at Sunday service are singing a hymn in chorus.

80. Teruko's bedroom

Teruko listens. The song gradually fades, transforming into a title.
Title: 'REJOICE YE MYRIADS! WHEN THE LORD JESUS DEFEATS THE KINGDOM OF THE DEAD, THE POWER OF DEATH WILL HAVE VANISHED, AND OUR LIVES WILL BE EVERLASTING.'
Teruko is deeply moved, and says to Yamashita:
'You know, for some reason I'm feeling better.'
Teruko appears happy, yet her face is still tinged with sorrow. Yamashita leads her to the

window.

Yamashita: 'Just look at that blue sky, those green trees!'

Title: 'EVERYWHERE THE WORLD IS CHARGED WITH THE VITALITY OF LIFE.'

81. (Insert) A blue sky

Two dogs come out of the forest and romp in the sunshine.

82. Back to Teruko's bedroom

Teruko feels increasingly happier. In due course, Yamashita says:

'I'll come again. Take good care of yourself.'
He leaves.

Teruko thanks him as she sees him off, and once again admires the view out the window.

(Close-up) Her face, lost in thought.

Yamashita's face comes to mind, but then again so does Yanagisawa's. Teruko resolves to do her best not to think of Yanagisawa.

83. Yanagisawa's room (night)

Yanagisawa returns home drunk, but he is definitely not happy in his drunken oblivion. He picks up the photo of an actress on his desk.

(Close-up of the actress's photograph.)

He then tears it up. In anguish, he takes a photo of Teruko from his desk drawer and stares at it. As he does so, Teruko appears before him and speaks to him. (Vision)

In frustration Yanagisawa buries his head in his hands. He then drinks some water from a pitcher beside him.

84. Yanagisawa's room (before noon)

Yanagisawa is now awake, brushing his teeth and washing his face. An elderly steward enters and sadly shows him an announcement in the newspaper.

(Newspaper announcement)

'AUCTION OF YANAGISAWA COLLECTION IN HAMACHO, NIHONBASHI WARD. BIDDING ON JULY 15TH AND 16TH. PREVIEWS IN THE MORNING, JULY 4TH AND 5TH.'

Steward: 'Sir, what is this announcement all about?'

Yanagisawa hesitates.

Yanagisawa: 'Oh, it's nothing, I'm just selling off some old things.'

Steward: 'But these are family heirlooms, left to you by your ancestors. Why are you doing this …?'

Yanagisawa: 'But I need the money. Why fuss over a few heirlooms?'

Steward: 'Sir, what a monstrous thought … but I suppose it can't be helped.'

The steward bows his head, balking at the very idea. Yanagisawa looks discomfited as he dries his face with a towel.

85. The garden of Teruko's house

Teruko's father is tending his flower garden. Teruko is playing quoits with her brother, Yo-chan; she sits down on a nearby fence and thinks for a moment.

(She recalls sailing with Yanagisawa) (Insert) But she shrugs it off as something that happened long ago. She then thinks of Yamashita. (With Yamashita, conducting an experiment) (Insert)

'Yamashita is the more manly of the two', she thinks.

Yo-chan: 'Sister, what are you thinking about? It's your turn.'

Teruko: 'Oh, so it is. I had completely forgotten.' She tosses another ring. Her father makes a strange face and laughs.

(Close-up) Teruko's father's face.

86. The laboratory

Yamashita is working in the laboratory with his assistant. Teruko suddenly visits the garden.

Teruko: 'May I come in?'

Yamashita: 'Teruko? Yes, please do. But it's very dirty in here.'

Teruko: 'What are you doing?'

Yamashita: 'This is radio-carbonium, a component for a wireless electric light. I'm nearly finished with my experiment, and if I'm successful.'

Teruko: 'Oh, my –'

Fig. 2. Harumi Hanayagi as Teruko and Minoru Murata as Yanagisawa in scene 89 of *The Glory of Life*. [Courtesy Kawakita Memorial Film Institute.]

Yamashita: 'Don't touch that, it's dangerous! It has an electric current running through it.'
Teruko: 'Don't frighten me so! Can I see it?'
She draws closer to look. The electric light has a phosphorescent glow. They both watch it.

87. Teruko's room (night)

Title: 'A STORMY NIGHT'
It is a stormy night. Teruko is in bed. There are lightning-flashes, and the sound of heavy rain.

88. Storm

Outdoors, cracks of lightning in the violent rainstorm. (Do something appropriate with this scene)

89. Teruko's room

A short while later, an anonymous figure shrouded in a black cloak enters the room. He walks across Teruko's room and approaches her bed.
(Close-up) Teruko is sleeping.
The man looks into Teruko's face, and at that very moment upsets a small figurine beside her. Surprised, the man tries to hide himself. Teruko wakes and switches on the lamp.
(Back)
She sees the person in black furtively standing in front of her bed and is about to scream. The man draws close to Teruko and places his hand over her mouth.
Yanagisawa: 'Please, wait – I'm not a thief!'
Then he pulls back the cloak's hood. Teruko, surprised, recognises Yanagisawa.

Teruko: 'Why have you come here? Please go away!'

Yanagiswa: 'No, I've come to offer you an apology.'

Yanagisawa speaks gently to Teruko. He sits in a chair by her side, and they are both silent for a moment.

Title: 'MISS SHIMAZAKI, I'VE COME TO APOLOGIZE TO YOU. I INTENDED ONLY TO LEAVE YOU THIS LETTER, I DID NOT MEAN TO WAKE YOU.'

He gives her the letter and buries his face in his hands. Teruko takes the letter over to the light and reads it.

(The contents of the letter) Insert …

Teruko: 'I understand …'

She runs her hand over Yanagisawa's head.

Title: 'UNTIL NOW I HAVE BEEN DELUDED. I AM LEAVING TO GO ABROAD …'

Teruko: 'I understand, please take good care of yourself.'

Her eyes glisten with tears.

Yanagisawa: 'From now on I intend to live an honest life.'

The two clasp hands, and then part.

Title: 'GOODBYE …'

Teruko weakly sits down on the bed as she watches Yanagisawa leave.

90. Storm

Violent wind and rain, cracks of lightening. Wrapped in his cloak, Yanagisawa vanishes into the darkness and the steadily falling rain.

91. On the mountain

Teruko and Yamashita are sitting on the mountainside.

Title: 'THE STORM HAS CLEARED'

Teruko: 'Did you know that Viscount Yanagisawa's son has gone abroad?'

She shows Yanagisawa's letter to Yamashita.

Yamashita: 'I received a letter as well.'

He takes a letter from Yanagisawa out of his pocket.

Yamashita: 'For the first time, he will live an honest life. I'm happy for him.'

Yamashita points in the distance.

(Insert) Smoke rises from the black chimney of a factory nestled in the hills.

They watch the rising smoke.

Title: 'THAT BLACK SMOKE REPRESENTS THE LIFE EACH ONE OF US HAS. IT IS ENERGY. LET US WORK, LET US FACE THE GLORY…'

92. The harbour

A steamship quietly leaves the harbour.

93. Aboard ship

Standing at the railing, Yanagisawa reluctantly watches the blue sky of his homeland recede in the distance. He takes off his hat and bows his head, his expression one of determination.

94. The sky at sunrise

The words 'Life is effort' appear in the sky at dawn. (Fade out).

Film History, Volume 9, pp. 388–409, 1997. Copyright © John Libbey & Company
ISSN: 0892-2160. Printed in Australia

Alias Jimmy Valentine *and* situational dramaturgy

Ben Brewster

This paper is drawn from work that Lea Jacobs and I have been engaged in for a number of years on the relation between the early cinema, and particularly the feature films of the 1910s, and nineteenth- and early twentieth-century theatre. Our starting point is the characterisation of that theatre by historians such as Michael Booth[1] as dominated by an aesthetics of spectacle. Unlike much contemporary film theory, however, we see spectacle not in opposition to narrative, but as implying a characteristic approach to narrative, which (developing an idea of Martin Meisel's)[2] we call 'situational'.

The notion of the dramatic situation is explored at greater length in our book *Theatre to Cinema: Stage Pictorialism and the Early Feature Film*,[3] but for present purposes, a 'situation' can be defined as a moment of stasis in the ongoing movement of a plot in which the forces moving the action in one direction and another are momentarily in balance or abeyance – moments of deadlock and suspense, but also ones of surprise. Such interruptions of the narrative flow shift the attention from the actions themselves to their causes and potential effects, and, in general, to the significance of the action as opposed to the action as such. Indeed, situational cause and effect is usually moral as much as or rather than physical, and moral contrast is one of the most typical features of situations. Situations thus have strong connotations; they subsume particular events under general schemata. When situations

have been noticed by theatre and film historians, it has usually been the ideological implications of these connotators that have been considered,[4] but here I would like to emphasise rather the formal effects of a situational dramaturgy. For example, situations help to organise the dramatic presentation of the narrative in time, providing alternations between movement and stasis, and ways of dividing a single causal chain into more convenient sub-units (on stage, the division into scenes and acts), these sub-units typically ending with a situation, whose resolution is delayed until the curtain rises again on a new act or scene. And they help to organise the action spatially, too, insofar as scene design and blocking are arranged to enable actors to reach the points of stasis in the action so that they form a composition which underscores the significance of the moment.

In nineteenth-century theatre, the most striking form taken by these temporal and spatial punctuations was a marked theatrical device, one very familiar to all theatrical practitioners: the 'tableau' or stage picture, the moment when all the actors on stage held a pose or attitude for a more or less long period. Consider the end of Act 5 Scene 3 of the

Ben Brewster is Assistant Director of the Wisconsin Center for Film and Theater Research. Correspondence c/o 6040 Vilas Hall, 821 University Avenue, Madison, Wisconsin 53706 USA.

George Aiken dramatisation of *Uncle Tom's Cabin* (1852). On Simon Legree's Red River plantation, Tom refuses to whip his fellow slave Emmeline. Legree orders his overseers, Sambo and Quimbo, to take Tom away and beat him for his refusal to follow orders. The final stage direction reads:

> Music. – SAMBO and QUIMBO seize TOM and drag him up stage. LEGREE seizes EMMELINE, and throws her round to R.H. – She falls on her knees, with her hands lifted in supplication. – LEGREE raises his whip, as if to strike TOM. – Picture. – Closed in.[5]

Thus, while the dialogue calls for Sambo and Quimbo to take Tom off stage and beat him, the tableau halts the action before their exit, and shows Legree himself about to administer the punishment, constituting a composite image at the expense of a linear presentation of the narrative events. Simple narrative logic is violated in order to provide the most effective visual summary of the conflicts that have been played out in the scene. The composite character of the image is also what gives the tableau its punctuating force.

More generally than the 'stage picture' *stricto sensu*, a situational dramaturgy gave rise to a pictorial conception of drama. In doing so, it drew on eighteenth-century reworkings of the problem of the relationship between painting and poetry, in particular of the representation of action (which unfolds in time) in the static media of painting and sculpture. Aristotle had dismissed the visual aspect of drama (*opsis* or spectacle) as 'having nothing to do with poetry', and this seemed to condemn visual representation to the role of a decorative adjunct to verbal imitation. Painting and sculpture were rescued from this degradation by an argument most cogently formulated by Lessing, who proposed in the *Laocoön* that the best kind of paintings could represent action by selecting 'the most fruitful moment' or the 'pregnant moment' to portray, a moment of harmonious repose which bore the traces of the processes that had brought it about (its causes) and the foreshadowing of its consequences (its effects). Thus paintings acquired the beginning, middle and end to constitute them as narratives in Aristotle's sense, and to rescue them from the charge of being mere 'opsis'.[6]

The stage pictures of nineteenth-century drama drew on this conception of the portrayal of action, and it is easy to see how such a conception of the picture accords with the notion of situation and the means of portraying it: a situation is a moment of repose at which it is possible to stand back and contemplate the significance of the elements at play, in particular their causes and effects. However, the application of this Aristotelian conception of painting as imitative of action to drama produced an anti-Aristotelian tendency in drama. Action as movement was arrested into action as simultaneously rendered causal sequence. The temporal foreshortening this demanded is illustrated in the example above. Although making his protection of Emmeline (rather than the incidental character Lucy, as in the novel) the immediate cause of Tom's beating tightens the causal links (since his later assistance in Emmeline's escape from the plantation leads to his death), the picture, which evokes the iconography of paintings of the scourging of Christ, represents the broader causal process of Tom's martyrdom at the hands of Legree more than it does the immediate one of Tom's part in the rescue of Emmeline from her master's sexual attentions. So while such pictorialism guarantees the intelligibility and significance of the action, it threatens the overall causal unity of the drama, since the causal connections are, so to speak, retracted into the series of pictures, a dislocation characteristically condemned, in Aristotelian terms, as 'episodic'.

Thus, a situational dramaturgy, although drawing on Aristotelian principles, tended to be at odds with the expectations articulated in most written and published theories and descriptions of drama, which were based on the representation of a closed and coherent causal chain, and emphasised the continuous rise and fall of dramatic excitement from the initial exposition through the climax to the dénouement. In addition, nineteenth-century theorists of drama, influenced by idealist philosophy, wished to stress the internal, spiritual aspects of action as opposed to merely external mechanical cause and effect, and therefore tried to locate the causal chain in character motivation. Hence they deplored the resort to external causes, and in particular, they deplored coincidence, the bringing about of narratively satisfying impasses and resolutions by arbitrary concatenations of external circumstances. A situational dramaturgy, to the contrary, rejoiced in coincidence, because it provided the opportunity for the assemblage of as disparate as possible material into a single picture, insofar as a whole series of causal chains converged on the one moment of stasis, and causes were largely external, and hence picturable elements.

As a result, in the nineteenth and early twentieth centuries, two only partly reconcilable theatrical discourses uneasily co-existed: an 'official' Aristotelian one, which dominated academic writing, indeed all abstract in-depth discussion of theatre; and a largely unself-conscious everyday situational one, found in writings which deal with local and practical theatrical matters such as technical problems of staging and acting, and also often in occasional theatrical writings such as reviews. The only sustained accounts of situational dramaturgy are hostile ones in the official discourses, or parodies. The importance of the notion of the situation in both the popular and the 'respectable' theatre contemporaneous with the rise of the feature film, and the ways a situational dramaturgy was adopted in the cinema to handle films which now had the length to emulate stage plays, is therefore easy to miss. In this paper, I shall attempt to illustrate situational dramaturgy at work in an early twentieth-century play, Paul Armstrong's *Alias Jimmy Valentine* (premièred at the Studebaker Theater, Chicago, 25 December 1909), and the film adaptation of it directed by Maurice Tourneur for World Film in 1915.[7]

Armstrong's play derives from a short story by O. Henry, *A Retrieved Reformation*, first published in *Cosmopolitan* magazine in 1903.[8] The staging that premièred at Chicago and then moved to Wallack's Theater in New York on 21 January 1910 was produced by Liebler & Co., directed by Edward E. Rose, and starred H.B. Warner as Jimmy.[9] Extracts from the play and synopses were published in contemporary magazines,[10] and I have seen four typescripts (prepared in both Chicago and New York) of slightly different versions in the Billy Rose Library in New York.[11] A French version of the play adapted by Yves Mirande and Henry Géroule as *Le Mystérieux Jimmy* was produced at the Théâtre de la Renaissance in Paris, premièring on 26 June 1911.[12] Tourneur later claimed that 'I produced the French stage version of *Alias Jimmy Valentine*'.[13] According to Jean Mitry, between 1910 and 1912, Tourneur worked as an actor and stage manager

for Abel Tarride, the actor-manager of the Théâtre de la Renaissance, and also directed some productions there, so the claim may well be correct.[14] I have not located a text of the French version, but from the detailed summary included in a review by Montcornet in *Le Théâtre*,[15] it is clearly close to a version premièred at El Teatre Principal, Barcelona, on 16 April 1912 in a Catalan translation (probably from the French) by Carles Costa as *El misteriòs Jimmy Samson*, which was published many years later.[16] The French and Catalan versions are fairly free adaptations, and it is possible that the French one influenced Tourneur or his uncredited screenwriter (if any) in the film adaptation. This was produced in 1915 by the World Film Corporation with Robert Warwick in the lead part.[17]

O. Henry's story is only a few pages long, and essentially presents a single situation: Jimmy Valentine, an expert safecracker, is released from prison, collects his burglar's tools, and travels to Elmore, Arkansas, where he plans to rob the bank. However, he falls in love with the bank manager's daughter, reforms, opens a shoe shop, prospers, and gets engaged to the girl he loves. A police detective with a warrant for his arrest arrives in Elmore just as Jimmy is preparing to leave for the West with his bride. At that moment it is discovered that her little niece has been shut into the new bank vault, which has a time lock. Jimmy uses his tools to open the safe and save the little girl, and the detective thereupon tears up the warrant, allowing Jimmy to marry and live happily ever after.

This account of the situation involves a lot of backstory; its bare bones is the ironic position Jimmy is placed in: if he rescues the little girl, he betrays his identity, is arrested, and his reform goes for nothing; if he sticks to his new persona, the little girl dies. This is a characteristic situation: the protagonist is confronted with a dilemma,[18] and the action is suspended to allow all its implications to be grasped; the dilemma poses two contrasting moral outcomes; it evokes the chains of circumstances that led to the protagonist's need to decide, and the possible future outcomes of his decision. Like most situations reduced to bare bones, it is not original. As Montcornet pointed out in *Le Théâtre*, it is the situation in *Les Misérables* that the escaped convict Jean Valjean finds himself in when, while disguised as M. Madeleine, the humanitarian mayor of Montreuil-sur-mer, he and his nemesis, the police detective Javert, are bystanders as père Fauchelevent is caught under a heavy cart; should he allow Fauchelevent to die, or raise the cart off him, revealing his great strength and thereby reinforcing Javert's already aroused suspicions as to his real identity?

This situation provides the climax and leads to the dénouement – acting out of character, the detective tears up the warrant – in all the versions of the *Alias Jimmy Valentine* story[19] and is consistently described in reviews in 'situational' language.[20] However, it is not enough to constitute a full-length stage play, which has to be divided into a number of acts, and, in situational dramaturgy, such acts have to have their own mini-climaxes and dénouements, i.e. their own secondary situations. As Tourneur remarked: 'Structurally there is no more resemblance between the O. Henry fiction and the Armstrong comedy than there is between a chess board and a woman weeping.'[21] Armstrong motivated the situation by providing a new and more complex chain of prior events, allowing for this series of climaxes. Before his arrival in the town where the action is set (Springfield, Illinois, in the various plays and films), Jimmy had met the banker's daughter, Rose Lane, before; he had rescued her from the attentions of a masher on a train, and in the resulting fight, the masher had fallen from the train and been so badly injured that he died, not before denouncing his assailant as a safecracker. Rose meets Valentine again when she is visiting Sing Sing prison with her uncle, the Deputy Governor of New York; Valentine has been jailed on the basis of the masher's testimony, but proclaims his innocence (and his inability to crack safes). On learning of his chivalrous action, Deputy Governor Fay believes his protestations and promises to get him a pardon; Rose subsequently persuades her father to give him a post in his bank in Springfield. Doyle, the detective who had got him convicted and vowed to nail him again after the pardon, traces him to Springfield and arrives with a warrant for another crime (committed in Springfield, Massachusetts). Valentine succeeds in bluffing Doyle with a carefully prepared alibi. The basic situation of the story then follows.

The action is distributed over four acts (though one typescript presents this as three acts, the last having two scenes, as the fourth act in the others is very short). The first act is set in the Warden's office in Sing Sing, with the visit of Rose, her uncle, and members of the prison reform league the Gate of Hope. The Warden offers his visitors an exhibition of criminal types, culminating in the request to Jimmy that he open a safe without knowing the combination, which he insists he is unable to do. Rose recognises Jimmy, and persuades her uncle to secure him a pardon. The second act takes place immediately after Jimmy's release, in a hotel lobby in Albany, where Jimmy has arranged to meet Rose. Jimmy is approached by Detective Doyle, but refuses to become a stool pigeon. Red Joclyn and Bill Avery, former associates of Jimmy's, appear, and Valentine tells them he is going straight (provoking a minor situation where he is nearly seduced back into crime by his former partners, to be discussed in more detail later). Rose introduces Jimmy to her father, and the latter, at her request, offers Jimmy a job in the Springfield bank. Jimmy promises to get Joclyn a job there too. The third act takes place in that bank several years later. Jimmy (going by the name Lee Randall) is now Lane's trusted right-hand man, and Joclyn is a watchman. Avery, who has reformed and married a widow whose son is a photographer, arrives with a photograph he has had made for Jimmy. Avery has been trailed by Doyle, who announces his imminent arrival. Jimmy decides to brazen out the situation, using the doctored photograph to establish an alibi. He is successful, but as the crestfallen Doyle prepares to leave, Red runs in calling 'Jimmy', to say that Kitty Lane has been locked into the safe. Act 4 (or Act 3, scene 2) is set in the vault. A blindfolded Jimmy opens the safe with Red's assistance, watched unbeknown to them by Doyle and Rose. When Jimmy takes off the blindfold he sees Doyle, and gives himself up. Rose comes forward and pleads for him; realising that the two are in love, Doyle tears up the warrant and leaves the couple together.

The problem with this structure is that it sags in the middle. The first act is fine, climaxing with the attempt by Warden Handler to persuade Jimmy to demonstrate his safecracking skills, Rose's revelation, and Fay's promise to have him pardoned; the third has Jimmy bluffing Doyle; and the fourth is the climactic situation; but the second only has the attempt by Joclyn and Avery to tempt Jimmy back to criminality. The French version of the play eliminates the second act, and Tourneur's film drastically cuts it. The French play has two acts in Jimmy's office in the bank before the final vault scene (here, too, Act 3, Scene 2), and adds a new character, a villain, to complicate the relations between Jimmy and his former associates on the one hand, and his dealings with the detective on the other. Act 2 reveals that Rose is engaged to a ne'er-do-well cousin, but has fallen in love with Jimmy. Evans (as the detective is called in the French and Catalan versions) tries to persuade Rose's father that Jimmy and his friends are untrustworthy, without success. Jimmy is unsure of the conversion of one of his associates (here called Dick le Rat) and leaves the office in darkness with the safe open. There is a scuffle in the darkness, and when Jimmy and the bank's owner return and turn the lights on again, $20,000 is missing, and Dick is unconscious on the floor. In Act 3, Scene 1, the banker wavers in his trust, but the cousin is later caught passing out forged banknotes, and Jimmy reveals that the money stolen from the safe was forged bills he had deliberately substituted for the real thing as a test for Dick's honesty. The cousin is sent packing, and the detective is baffled, but then Kitty is found to have been locked in the safe, and scene 2 is the standard climax and dénouement. The obvious weakness of this solution is the loss of the bluffing scene, as well as something curiously old-fashioned in the introduction of a conventional villain in addition to the more ambiguous nemesis figure of the detective (though perhaps there is another Hugolian precedent in the doubling of Javert by Thénardier).

The film follows some of the changes introduced into the French version, notably the conflation of Lieutenant Governor Fay and Rose's father Lane, and the virtual elimination of Act 2 (reduced to two short scenes in a bar sandwiching a third in Fay's house). This creates some problems: it makes sense that Jimmy, with a former criminal associate in tow, would stop off in Albany to thank his benefactor en route from Sing Sing to New York city, but not that he should travel all the way to Illinois for the same purpose; and it is unclear how the lieutenant governor of another state would have the power in Sing Sing that Fay is supposed to have. This would not worry a Parisian audience, who probably had no idea where either Springfield is, or of the status of a lieutenant governor of an American state, but it

might seem a problem for American spectators (though I have no knowledge of adverse critical comment about the film on these grounds at the time). The key situation in Act 2, the moment when Jimmy's associates try to persuade him back to a life of crime, is shifted by Tourneur into what in the American play is Act 3, in Jimmy's Springfield office, again following the French adaptation's model of boosting the incidents in Act 3.

A much more important change in the film is in the exposition. Whereas O. Henry's story begins with Jimmy's release from prison, and the first scene in both the American and French versions of the play is set in the Warden's office in Sing Sing while he is serving his sentence, the 1915 film begins by establishing Lee Randall, alias Jimmy Valentine, as a safe cracker, showing him and his associates Red, Avery, and Cotton carrying out a bank robbery, and their pursuit by Detective Doyle. There follows a direct representation of the incident with Jimmy, Cotton (the masher) and Rose on the train, Cotton's confession, Jimmy's arrest and his arrival in Sing Sing.

In directly representing what was backstory in the play, Tourneur is following standard prescriptions of the period. It was generally agreed that whereas in literature it was possible to double back in time and tell earlier events after later ones, this was inappropriate in drama and film, where all significant narrative action should be portrayed in story order.[22] Nevertheless, *in medias res* openings were highly valued. In the live theatre, these two requirements were reconciled by resort to expository dialogue, in which characters tell each other the crucial information about the past, allowing a reasonably rapid move to interesting action.[23] In film, this reconciliation was less felicitous, since, at least in the early 1910s, lengthy titles early in a film were frowned on (subsequently they became more possible, and many early 1920s films have quite extensive narrative titles at the beginning). Exposition in 1910s features is therefore often clumsy, involving whole reels with no significant actions as who is who and how they are related is established. Staging a robbery almost immediately after the opening credits and doing so in a highly spectacular way, is Tourneur's solution to this problem.

It is a solution achieved at some cost, it should be said. For the whole first act of Armstrong's play,

Jimmy asserts his innocence of the crime for which he is in Sing Sing; not until his meeting with Red and Avery in Albany in Act 2 is it made explicit that he really is a safecracker. The uncertainty about this, together with the sincerity of Warner's performance,[24] helped evade a problem inherent in the story, that a character meant to be sympathetic to the audience persistently lies to his girlfriend and benefactors. In the film, he even appears fairly cynical. In turn this affects the relation between the film and its theme, the conversion of criminals. Contemporary reviews related the play to progressive reform (despite, or perhaps rather under the cover of, its ridicule of the reforming ladies of the Gate of Hope); it was seen as hard on crime when compared with romanticised stories and plays with criminal heroes like Raffles and Arsène Lupin, but nevertheless as proposing that, accorded fair treatment, 'non-degenerate' criminals (as opposed to figures like Blinky Davis and Dick the Rat, exhibited by Warden Handler to his visitors in Act 1) can be persuaded to reform.[25] Thus, as a way to set up a dilemma for the dénouement, 'going straight' carries considerable ideological baggage. In the film, by contrast, Jimmy's speeches about the joys of honest living, necessarily rather summary as dialogue titles, seem weak compared with the visual presentation of actual crime (there is no on-stage crime in the American version of the Armstrong play – indeed, although the story makes no sense unless Valentine is a criminal, no particular crime, apart from the death of Cotton, is unequivocally attributed to him).

More significant about the opening from the point of view of situational dramaturgy and the way it was adapted to the early feature film is the staging of the bank robbery scene. This involves the use of a multiple-room set, with the various rooms in the bank all visible simultaneously.

After a credit sequence with a portrait of Lee Randall and a dissolve to Jimmy in convict garb, Randall is seen leaving his office and going to an apartment in a poor quarter, setting his alarm clock and going to sleep. Waking at midnight, he goes to a rendezvous in waste ground with two accomplices, Red Joclyn and Bill Avery. Outside a bank they meet the fourth member of the gang, Cotton. While Avery stays outside as lookout, the other three men enter the bank by a back-alley basement en-

trance. So far the film has used a découpage with shots of moderate length simply following the principal actors, usually with somewhat elliptical connections between the shots, and only minimal alternation for the scenes of the two rendezvous. As soon as Valentine, Red and Cotton disappear down the basement trap-door and Avery settles to wait as lookout, the whole of the bank interior is shown in a single bird's-eye view, not from directly above but obliquely, and at an angle to the prevailing direction of the walls. As this is the double-height ground floor of a bank, the walls we can see the tops of might just plausibly be partitions that do not reach all the way to the ceiling (though if so they have very unfinished tops). Even so, it looks impossible for a camera actually in a real bank to have such a comprehensive view of all the interior spaces. Throughout the subsequent robbery, this is the only view of the ground-floor bank interior that we get, apart from one final closer view of the tellers' counter.

Although the action is quite fast, it is choreographed to produce a series of attitudes, with all the actors freezing when each door in the set is opened, as the thieves wait to be sure no one has seen or heard them (Figs 1–5). When they reach the safe, Jimmy and Red light a dark lantern and start to work on it (Fig. 6), while Cotton goes back to the door front right by which they entered to keep watch (Fig. 7). There is a cutaway to Avery watching (this cutaway covers the lengthy business of finding the safe combination and opening the safe), then we return to the original framing with the safe open and Cotton ferrying loot from it to Red at the door. As he hands Red a tray of valuables, Cotton drops it, and all freeze (Fig. 8). Cutaway to a close-up of a watchdog barking, then to Avery hearing it, then to a watchman waking up, back to the dog, back to the bird's-eye-view of the bank with the three burglars still frozen in position as before. There follow another shot of Avery, and two more shots of the watchman getting up and turning on the lights, then back to the bird's eye view, with the bank now lit, but mysteriously empty. The watchman enters and cautiously explores most of the rooms visible, finding nothing amiss, but at last he is set on by Cotton who has been hiding behind one of the doors of the room behind the tellers' counter. Jimmy and Red enter from their hiding place inside the safe and go to Cotton's assistance. Breaking free, the watchman

Fig. 1.

Fig. 2.

Fig. 3.

draws a gun and pursues the burglars through various doors (Fig. 9), until they manage to lock him into the room behind the counter. As they escape the way they entered, he comes to front left. Cut to a close shot of him blowing a whistle. After a short sequence showing Avery spotted, pursued and arrested by three policemen alerted by the whistle, we see the other three re-emerge from the basement trapdoor and run off.

Although the high-angle viewpoint is unprecedented on the live stage, the multiple-room set formed part of the tradition of spectacular staging. Hassan El Nouty makes it one of the centre-pieces of an argument that the nineteenth-century popular theatre aspired to a spatial realism and ubiquity that only the cinema could achieve. Both before and after, theatrical action was conceived of as taking place on the stage, with the diegetic space indicated rather than illusorily represented; only in this period was the spectator supposed to disavow the fact and see the represented rather than the real space. However, fictional actions demand much more spatial variety than a simple realistic stage setting can represent; hence the resort to the multiple-room set. But this set remains a compromise; the ambition is only achievable in the cinema, where the screen creates a much more purely fictional space, and one that can include any place whatsoever, simply by cutting from one scene to another *ad libitum*.[26]

If El Nouty is correct, one would expect multiple-room sets not to occur in the cinema, or to disappear rapidly once filmmakers realised the greater effectivity of scene-to-scene cutting for the same situations. However, in the light of the principles of situational dramaturgy outlined above, multiple-room sets would seem more than a halting step towards integral spatial realism; they enable all the elements of a complex situation to be staged at once in a single composite picture. The persistence of multi-room sets in the cinema would suggest that the exigencies of situations rather than those of realism dominate dramaturgy in both theatre and film in the first decades of the twentieth century.

El Nouty's case would seem to be borne out by developments in the one-reel film between 1907 and 1913. Multiple-room sets are found quite frequently in films made before 1910 for the representation of simultaneous actions in different but adjacent spaces. In the films produced by the Vitagraph Company of America between 1906 and 1908, such a set is probably the commonest way to represent a character in one room overhearing something in the next, e.g. in *Foul Play* (1907), *Father's Quiet Sunday* (1907) and *Circumstantial Evidence* (1908). However, even in these years the alternative of a cut from a view of one space to one of another was possible. By 1908, Vitagraph films regularly use room-to-room cutting for more or less simultaneous action in different adjacent spaces, e.g. in *The Boy, the Bust, and the Bath*. There are no multiple-room sets in the films copyrighted by the company in 1909. In most American films by the beginning of the 1910s, interior scenes are characteristically presented via alternating series of shots in adjacent rooms, and parallel or converging actions in different spaces more generally by repeated alternation between shots of each space.

Thus far, in El Nouty's terms, a theatrical simultaneity has been succeeded by a cinematic fragmentation and linearisation. And indeed, alternation of this kind remains one of the key ways of emphasising the simultaneity of differently located actions in the cinema. In a sense this extends the plausible space of the stage picture, allowing the

Fig. 4.

Fig. 5.

Fig. 6.

Fig. 7.

Fig. 8.

Fig. 9.

assemblage of contrasting elements without arbitrarily freezing the action into the kind of act-end *tableau* illustrated from the Aiken version of *Uncle Tom's Cabin* above. However, the option of alternation did not spell the end of the multiple-room set in the cinema. On the contrary, the early feature seems to have given it a new life. *Alias Jimmy Valentine* is not an isolated exception. A year later, Maurice Tourneur's set designer Ben Carré built a nine-room house set, with all the rooms on one side of a house visible simultaneously or separately, for a now lost film, *The Hand of Peril* (1916).[27] Two-room sets are found in German features such as *Zweimal gelebt* (d. Max Mack, 1912) and *Die Sumpfblume* (d. Viggø Larsen, 1913) and the Swedish *Havsgamar* (d. Victor Sjöström, 1916).

In *Alias Jimmy Valentine*, the multiple-room set is exploited for its spectacular effect, even in a context in which simultaneity via editing is standard. (Compare the cutaways to Avery, the barking dog, and the nightwatchman, followed by the cut back to the frozen burglars.) By showing a complex spatial layout as a whole, the divided set aids the suspense of the tiptoed break-in and the subsequent search by the nightwatchman. It also makes the movements of the characters from space to space comprehensible in a way which would have been extremely difficult if no view exceeded the visible space of a single room. It allows the burglary to be presented as a kind of ballet. This reinforces the film's already noted tendency to present crime as a jubilatory exercise of skill, its visual celebration of it undermining the lofty morality of intertitle speeches.

The suspenseful wait while the nightwatchman searches for the criminals – emphasised by the mysterious disappearance of the burglars who froze when Cotton dropped the tray and were still in the same positions in the next return to the bank interior – is a typical situation, but this does not seem to be the principal motivation for the bird's-eye-view staging. This scene, and everything which follows up to Detective Doyle's discovery of the dropped cufflink that implicates Jimmy in the robbery, is exposition. It is pictorial and situational, but it relates not so much to the tradition of the stage tableau, typically forming the climax or the end of a scene, but to that of the elaboration of a spectacular setting on the raising of a curtain; for example, the beginning of the slave-auction scene in *Uncle Tom's Cabin* (usually accompanied by songs and dances from the slaves awaiting sale), or the opening of Act 2 of Donizetti's opera *Lucia di Lammermoor* (where an orchestral interlude parallels the moonlit fountain visible on the stage for some time before any characters enter). It can be thought of as an expansion of the opening dissolve between Lee Randall and Jimmy Valentine. It offers a general view of crime before introducing the particular story of the hero.

A more typical situation, though one of fairly low intensity, is handled in the film version of *Alias Jimmy Valentine* by what is in some sense a characteristically 'cinematic' mode of editing: a 'vision' represented by an alternation between shots of a character and shots of his vision. This handling can nevertheless be shown to derive very directly from the way the incident was staged in the play. This is what I shall call the 'temptation scene', when Avery and Red try to persuade Jimmy to return to a life of crime by reminding him of what he will miss if he goes straight.[28]

In the American play, this scene, or moment in a scene, occurs in Act 2, in the lobby of a hotel in Albany after Jimmy's release from Sing Sing. Rose Lane and her father have arranged to meet Jimmy there. Jimmy is introduced to Lane, but then Lane and his daughter leave, Rose telling Jimmy to wait for her return. Jimmy talks to ladies of the prison reform group the Gate of Hope. Rejecting their offers of jobs, Jimmy says goodbye to the ladies, and Red Joclyn enters and greets him as an old associate, proposing a safe-cracking job he has staked out for him. Jimmy is unenthusiastic, and Red accuses him of deserting his old friends. They are joined by Avery, who is also disappointed to discover that Jimmy is going straight. When police

detective Doyle appears, Red and Avery hide. Doyle tells Jimmy he is after him for a burglary in Springfield, Massachusetts, but will forget it in exchange for information, particularly if Jimmy will turn in Avery. Jimmy refuses, and Doyle leaves. Red and Avery re-emerge, and point out to Jimmy how hard it will be for him to go straight with Doyle as an enemy. Jimmy is firm. Red guesses that Rose has something to do with his decision, and says he has seen Rose and her father in the station buying tickets to leave town; he surmises that Doyle has already spoken to them and alienated Rose's feelings for Jimmy. Jimmy wavers, and Red and Avery proceed to remind him of the excitement of their criminal life:

> **RED**: You ain't going to lose that coin I've got staked out for an hour's work? Seven thousand if there's a dime.
>
> **VAL**: Yes, I'll lose that.
>
> **AVERY**: And a trip abroad to brace you up after stir.
>
> **VAL**: (Sit.) Yes, I lose that too.
>
> **RED**: (L. of V.) But you won't lose the old thrill of going into a bank just before dawn, landing the watchman and feeling out the combination in the dark?
>
> **AVERY**: (R. of V.) And hearing the coppers pass and try the door?
>
> **RED**: And seeing the old safe open up like an oyster, and grabbing the dough?
>
> **AVERY**: And making a clean get-away?
>
> **RED**: And the long jump and the landing in at a swell cafe, Jimmie – eating the breakfast of a millionaire.
>
> **AVERY**: With the coin in your kick.
>
> **RED**: And reading the papers and laughing our heads off at what suckers we made of the coppers – you ain't going to lose that Jimmy?
>
> **VAL**: You got to me Red. Where is this lay-out you got? Can we get to it tonight?

However, a message arrives from Rose indicating that she and her father had simply gone to the station to reserve sleepers for the evening; she still expects to see him that afternoon. He returns to his resolution to go straight, and when Rose and her father reappear, the latter offers him a cashier's post in his bank in Springfield, Illinois. Jimmy takes it, and when the Lanes have gone, persuades Avery

Fig. 10.

to take one of the positions offered him by the Gate of Hope, and Red to follow him to Springfield where, in time, he will get him a job in the bank, too.

This is the version of the incident in three of the four typescripts of the play I have seen. In the fourth, which seems to be the earliest version (the opening exposition in incidental dialogue in the Sing Sing Warden's office and other moments such as this one are less carefully worked out), no dialogue is given to Avery, and there is no indication of the way Avery and Red station themselves on either side of Valentine to allow him no escape from their persuasions. Contemporary press photographs indicate that this is how it was staged in the New York production (Fig. 10).[29]

As I have noted, this is not a climactic situation like the final vault opening scene. It is of considerable moment, however, given the importance of the theme of reformation in the play. The seriousness and difficulty of the question is indicated by one of the Billy Rose Library typescripts – neither the one quoted from nor the putatively 'earliest' version, but one which, from the complex set of 'doublings' of the parts in its cast list, was presumably for a travelling production, and hence one that would have had to have been seen by more provincial audiences than that of the Studebaker or Wallack's. Whereas all the other scripts end the second act on a light touch ('RED: What do I do? VAL: You trail along, Red. Get a job in my town for a year and by

that time I'll have one for you. RED: Doing what? VAL: I'm going to make you watchman in a National Bank. (Curtain)'), this script has a Salvation Army chorus off singing 'Rock of Ages', reminding Red of his old mother ('RED: How I would like to see her now. VAL: She sees you Red. RED: Do you think so Jimmy. Do you think so. If she does, I want her hand to guide me to that better world.' (Sits at VAL's feet. Chorus continues for curtain. RED looking at VAL at drop.)') The audiences for this version were clearly expected to need convincing that the heroes' move from crime to respectability involved a true conversion.

In the 1915 film, the temptation scene is moved to what in the play is Act 3, in Lee Randall's office in the bank in Springfield, Illinois. Jimmy is head cashier and Red commissionaire at the National Bank, and Avery pays them his first visit since their arrival in Springfield. The office set has two wood-panelled walls at right-angles; in this scene, one wall runs from midground left to rear centre, the other rear centre to front right (echoing the play's 'office set on the angle'). There are double doors rear left, a door midground right, and (although we do not see it in this scene) a door off front right. Jimmy's desk is front left facing left, with his chair therefore more or less front centre. This framing is maintained throughout the temptation scene, the other shots being intertitles or cutaways.

After Red arrives and announces Avery, the latter enters, and, after greeting his old friends, walks round the office, obviously 'casing the joint'. When Jimmy insists that he has no intention of robbing the bank, and Red rather ruefully confirms this, Jimmy sits front centre at his desk looking towards camera, Red looks off left, and Avery turns and looks off right (i.e. none is looking at either of the others). All pause, sunk in thought. Avery smiles, comes further forward, puts his right hand on Jimmy's left shoulder, gazes towards camera, and speaks (Fig. 11). A title follows: 'Remember, Jimmy, the old thrills of the past ...' In the return to the scene, Red, Jimmy and Avery register excitement as they remember. There is fade out, then a fade up on a circular vignette of two of them peering out of a basement

Fig. 11.

Fig. 12.

Fig. 13.

window while Red stands outside on watch (Fig. 12). A fade out and in returns to the scene, and the characters regroup, still holding basically the same positions. They freeze again (Fig. 13), and another scene from the past is inserted (Fig. 14), framed by fades as before. The same thing happens four times, with Red taking over from Avery the narrator's role midway through (Figs 15–18).[30] On the last return to the scene, Jimmy grabs Red's left hand and Avery's right, sits on the desk and starts to promise to go back to the old ways. However, Rose and her little sister and brother enter, Jimmy is reminded of his resolution, and (in a title) vows to go straight, come what may.

It is obvious how closely Tourneur follows the stage version here, even to the gesture of Jimmy grasping both his companions' hands at the point where he almost succumbs (not noted in any of the scripts, but shown in the published photograph).[31] The only difference is that Red and Avery sit stage right and left, respectively, i.e. the other way round from the film. In the temptation scene, the dialogue of the stage version is replaced more or less speech for speech (though not quite in the same order) by visions: 'Hearing the coppers pass and try the door ... seeing the old safe open up like an oyster and grabbing the dough ... landing in at a swell cafe ... eating the breakfast of a millionaire ... laughing our heads off at what suckers we made of the coppers.' Isolating visions as separate shots introduced by fades out and in was by this time a standard convention in the cinema, replacing the earlier, more directly stage-derived convention of superimposing the vision in part of the scene showing the character whose vision it is (the Vitagraph 1907 adaptation of *The Bells – Retribution, or, The Brand of Cain* – replaces the back wall of the inn with a snowscape for Mathias's vision of his

Fig. 14.

Fig. 15.

Fig. 16.

murder of the Polish Jew many years earlier, just as Irving's famous production did, although the sink and rise used by Irving was presumably replaced by a stop-motion substitution).[32] The difference between the stage and screen versions of this scene is not without its effect – once again, the visual presentation of the thrills of crime tends to outweigh the titles' verbal insistence on the greater attractiveness of going straight. Nevertheless, in both versions a narrative situation gives rise to a pictorial presentation, and the stage presentation of that situation provides the basic framework for that in the film, notwithstanding the very different nature of the space carved out by the moving-picture camera and the possibilities offered by editing.

The climax in the film might seem much less similar to the stage versions. What is a single scene, and a short one, in all versions of the play, is divided into some 58 shots in the surviving print of the film.[33] Moreover, unlike the scenes already discussed, the large number of shots and titles also involves a variety of shot scales and camera angles, not simply cutaways from a single basic scene framing to simultaneous events elsewhere, or vision scenes.

The film introduces the last scene via an alternation, intercutting the final stages of the confrontation between Valentine and Doyle with Banker Fay's departure, and Bobby and Kitty playing hide-and-seek in the vault by the new safe. As Doyle is stumped by the doctored photograph, Kitty hides in the safe, and Bobby closes and locks the door on her. Doyle gives up and takes his leave of the supposed Lee Randall, exiting by a rear right door. Jimmy exults. After a shot of Kitty from inside the safe, we return to the office, and Red runs in the front right door, which, when open, blocks the door through which Doyle left. After a title in which Red indicates that the combination is unknown, we return to the scene, with Bobby also on (the ellipsis suggests missing footage). After agonising, Jimmy responds to their pleading, takes off his coat, and all three run off through the front right door. It closes, revealing Doyle in the half-open rear right door. Doyle comes forward, smiles sardonically, and follows the others off front right. A brief sequence shows Fay on the train, where he reads the combination. Jimmy and Red then enter a long shot of the vault from the left, and set to work to open it (this I have taken rather arbitrarily as the 'first' shot of the final scene).

Fig. 17.

Thus the film sets up the final situation by suspense, anticipating the reversal of Jimmy's fortunes simultaneously with his successful bluffing of Doyle. The plays, on the contrary, present a surprise reversal (although, of course, the fact that the children are playing in the vault near a new safe whose combination has not yet been set is established near the beginning of Act 3). The Act ends with Red shouting 'Jimmy', which is heard by the departing Doyle, who waits as the curtain falls. The scripts indicate 'curtain', but it is not impossible that an open-stage scene change with lowered lights was anticipated, as the Act 3 corner set of Lee

Fig. 18.

Randall's office was intended to be set up inside the vault set of Act 4, and could be removed, probably flown, very rapidly. Whatever scene change method was used, the transition was intended to be as brief as possible, to avoid dissipating the tension engendered by the surprise. The Wallack's playbill indicated that 'between Acts III and IV there will be an interval of but one minute'.[34] Rapid scenic transformations of this kind were a regular feature of situational theatre; the reviewer of the play in the *New York Dramatic Mirror* makes this rapidity in some sense the cause of the situation:

> One of the tensest situations imaginable is produced when the scene magically changes to

the cellar of the bank, and Randall accompanied by the bank watchman is seen in a state of feverish excitement working in the semi-gloom to open the combination by the phenomenal sense of feeling with which nature has endowed him. From an open door the sleuth is seen watching the efforts of his prey, while in another door, contemplating the scene, stands Rose.[35]

Alternation is, in a sense, the cinematic equivalent of a sudden scene change. Such changes in the theatre impress because of their apparent difficulty. The ease with which films can cut soon destroyed the magical quality of the transition; the alternation as it were resists this attrition by multiplying the number of changes. However, in this case it does tend to undermine the suspense of the bluffing scene by anticipating the next crisis.

The *New York Dramatic Mirror*'s comment describes the climactic situation as a picture. It also draws attention to two other features of the theatrical presentation of this picture: the lighting, and the stage grouping. The main business of the scene consists in the blindfolded Jimmy, assisted by Red, sandpapering his fingers and then turning the knob of the safe to feel the tumblers and thus find the combination. In the film version, the main changes in shot scale in the scene involve this action. When Red and Jimmy enter the vault, the safe is at the rear of a long shot. After a title and return to scene, there is a cut-in to a medium long shot. Later, two slightly different medium-shot framings are used, and in the middle of the sequence (the 26th of 58 shots) there is a close-up showing solely the hands of Red and Jimmy as Jimmy turns the knob and Red lights matches to read the number. Framings then return to medium shot, and to medium long shot when the safe is opened and Kitty falls out, unconscious.

In the play the same effect of concentration on the safe door and the knob was achieved by lighting. One of the playtexts has a lighting plot for Act 4 as follows:

> Blue foots and border down to 3–4 and as Jimmy says: 'Close the blind, I can't work in the light' then as Red pulls down blind, lower the lights to 1–4 and throw on the spot from the baby, which is placed in the Center of the trough and worked from the board, this is pointed so as to train on the safe door, and make about a four foot spot, outside the window is an amber flood which goes down with the lowering of the shade. At the entrance of Doyle gradually bring up the blue foots and as the child falls out of the safe door, start up the blue border and strips, and pull the spot so that gradually the lights are full up in the blues and stand so for the rest of the act.

The script itself gives a slightly different cue for the spot:

> **VAL**: Come on, blindfold me, the old gag. (Red does so and leads him to vault ...)

RED: (Kneeling at safe) Hurry, Jimmy, that kid. [...]
RED: (Lights match) Ten ... My God, I heard that baby scream. [...]
VAL: I heard it too. Here we are again – match.
RED: (Lights match – SPOT) Forty-two.
VAL: That's it, forty-two, that's what it should be ... keep your nerves, pal – there – match.

Ostensibly the darkening of the vault is to help Jimmy concentrate on his fingers, and the spot might seem to be a representation of Red's matchlight. However, Jimmy is blindfolded from the beginning of the scene, making the lowered blinds somewhat redundant, and Red has already lit a match before the one that constitutes the cue for the spot; the function of the lighting here is more to orchestrate the situation than it is to represent a realistic environment. It is noticeable that, able to use change in shot scale for this orchestration, the film dispenses with all lighting effects, showing the vault at the same lighting level as the scenes in the office, keeping to that level for the whole scene, and not even attempting to indicate the light from Red's matches with a practical arc or baby spot. The video version, which is coloured to reproduce the tinting and toning of the nitrate original, has no colour effects in this scene either.[36]

In the play, Doyle enters stage right almost as soon as Red and Jimmy are engrossed in their attempt to open the safe; he stands in the doorway until the safe is open and Red has taken Kitty to a doctor. Rose (who is unaware of Kitty's predicament) enters stage left some time after Doyle, to find Jimmy apparently robbing the bank. She then sees Doyle, and is about to intervene (to warn Jimmy?), but a gesture from Doyle stops her. She stands stage left until the safe is open. The scene most frequently used in the contemporary press to illustrate reviews of *Alias Jimmy Valentine* is the resulting group, with Doyle to the left, Rose to the right, and Red and Jimmy at the safe in the centre (Fig. 19).[37]

The film follows this arrangement of entrances and groupings precisely, but fragments it into a series of framings. Unlike all the other editing patterns in the film, this one also involves a change of angle. After the opening long shot of the vault in which Jimmy sandpapers his hands and starts to try the knob, and the cut-in to a medium long shot in which he is blindfolded by Red, there is a cut to an oblique long shot from the left, with stairs leading up to the bank rear right, the safe midground left, and a wall front left. Doyle enters front left and stands there looking at the pair by the safe. Subsequently there are a series of cutaways from the medium shots of Red and Jimmy at work on the safe to medium shots of Doyle watching them off right (these filmed frontally). A return to the same oblique long shot shows Rose enter down the stairs right, and find Jimmy at the safe (Fig. 20). There follow frontal medium shots of Rose watching Jimmy off left, and expressing disillusionment and grief (Fig. 21). In an alternation of medium shots, Rose then sees Doyle (also off left), but her glance is directed more to the front (Fig 22), and goes to speak, but Doyle lifts a warning finger (Fig. 23) and she remains quiet (Fig. 24). After a return to the oblique long shot, there follows a series of shots of Red and Jimmy (and a cutaway to Kitty inside the safe), punctuated by returns to the medium shots of Doyle and Rose. The print then finishes as follows:

Fig. 19.

Fig. 20.

50 MLS As 4. The door of the safe. Red and Jimmy open it. Kitty falls out and off bottom of screen left. Red picks her up. Jimmy tells him to take her to a doctor, and he exits right toward the stairs off. Jimmy takes off the blindfold, looking down left, expressing quiet satisfaction. Pan right to bring on Rose right, who approaches and reaches out a hand, but does not touch him. He is unaware of her. Jimmy looks at his hands, then slowly raises his eyes and looks off left at Doyle. His smile vanishes.

51 MS As 7. Parallel view of area to the left of the safe. Doyle looking off right. He raises his left hand and points at Jimmy off.

52 MLS As 4. Jimmy looks off left, as does Rose. Jimmy expresses resignation, drops his hands.

53 MS As 7. Doyle exits right.
54 MLS As 4. Doyle enters left, raising handcuffs. Rose comes forward and pleads with Doyle. Jimmy sees her for the first time, and leans back in despair. He asks her: 'Did you see it all?' She nods. Doyle lowers cuffs and gets warrant out of inside pocket. Jimmy asks Rose for the rose she is wearing in her lapel. She unpins it and gives it to him, he kisses it. Doyle follows the train of gestures with his eyes. Jimmy turns to Doyle and offers his hands for the cuffs. Doyle stops him, and indicates Rose ('You are in love?'). Rose nods and pleads with Doyle again. Doyle looks up, ponders a moment, then tears up the warrant. Jimmy realises

Fig. 21.

Fig. 22.

what is happening and asks Doyle if he is to go free. Doyle nods, says goodbye to them both, and exits left.

55 MS As 7. Doyle already on. He turns back to right, waves his left finger, and speaks.

56 Title: '... but just to retain your respect; don't think I fell for that fake picture'.

57 MS As 7. Doyle smiles, then turns and exits left.

58 MLS As 4. Rose looks down off right, drained, as Jimmy looks off left after Doyle. Jimmy starts to turn back to Rose. Freeze frame and fade out [presumably restoration artifacts replacing a lost final reconciliation].

Compare this with the play:

(Dog heard to lift inside [the safe]. Valentine opens door. As the safe door opens, Kitty falls out. Red picks her up.)
RED: She's dead.
VAL: No, she'll be all right in five minutes. Take her to the doctor on the corner.
(Red carries Kitty toward door Left, meets Rose.)
ROSE: Kitty – hurry.
RED: She'll be all right in a few minutes.
VAL: I beat you – I beat you ... (Bus.) (Seeing Doyle) I guess you win after all. I'll go without ...
DOYLE: There's someone there that might want to say goodbye to you. (Indicates Rose. Valentine turns and sees her.)
VAL: You saw, God! (Rose nods and starts toward him. He looks at her, then Doyle, crosses to Rose and takes a rose from her breast.) You won't mind my having that flower I know. I am going to be gone a long time, and this I want you to know and remember through the years, my love for you is the only clean thing I ever knew, and it will never, never end. (Turns to Doyle)
DOYLE: Didn't you have an engagement with the lady?
ROSE: Yes, he did. An engagement that means my happiness, my life and his.
DOYLE: Then I guess we'll just cheat the state of Massachussets.
VAL: You mean that, Doyle? (Going C)
DOYLE: Oh Jimmy, you had me going all right, but just to retain your respect, don't think I fell for that double negative photograph. Goodbye. (Exit R)
VAL: (Turning to Rose) You know who that was?
ROSE: I only know that I love you.
VAL: You love me now that you know?
ROSE: Perhaps I always knew. If a woman loves, she rejects that which does not fit into her dreams, but if she loves as I ...
VAL: I'll make good, Rose, I'll make good.
                    CURTAIN

Apart from the omission by the film (that is, the surviving print of the film) of the brief dialogue about Kitty between Red and Rose, play and film are identical gesture for gesture – indeed, the actors in the film clearly speak the shorter passages of dialogue in the play. Only the cutting to medium shots of Doyle (and Rose, before the pan right and her movement towards Jimmy that bring them together in shot 50) is different. Note that the shot change is not needed to isolate significant actions by the characters. The play characteristically relays gestures from character to character, so that when one has business the others remain relatively still, ensuring that the audience does not miss a significant gesture. Thus, once Red and Jimmy's activity by the safe is established, Doyle makes his entrance and stands to the left. He remains stationary as Rose enters on the right, sees Jimmy, then sees Doyle, and starts to speak. She freezes while Doyle makes his warning gesture. Both remain still until the safe is open and Red has left with Kitty. Rose, then Doyle, then move into the centre towards Jimmy. Significant turning points in the action never compete for attention, nor would they have done in the film in a very long shot showing all the characters.

Fig. 23.

Fig. 24.

What the editing does here is to supply the width of the stage. The proscenium opening of the Studebaker was 36-feet wide, that of Wallack's 34.[38] By contrast, film screens at this period rarely exceeded fifteen feet in width, even in a large theatre.[39] Thus, particularly given the low light on most of the stage, it was quite plausible for the play to have Doyle and Rose flank Red and Jimmy unseen for a large part of the scene (in the published photographs showing this composition, such as figure 19, they may well have been brought closer in than they were during performance to help page design in the magazines for which these photographs were intended). Given the small size of the cinema screen, Tourneur had four options in the film. He could use a very long shot including all the characters throughout the scene (as in the bank robbery scene); but individual characters' different responses to the event constitute the situation here, requiring a clear view of facial expressions (unlike the bank robbery, where only an external action was at stake). He could bring Doyle and Rose much closer to Red and Jimmy, allowing a medium long shot framing; but then their undetected presence would strain plausibility.[40] He could use an oblique angle with one of the line of characters close to the camera and the furthest far away, as he does in shots 5, 15, and 24 (which explains the otherwise rather remarkable change of camera angle in a film which does not regularly resort to such editing devices); but if held for the whole scene this framing would unduly privilege the figure with his back to the audience (and hence a less visible face) while reducing the background figure to illegible proportions. Or he could use editing to ensure equally close framings of all the characters. Obviously, the last is the option Tourneur took. He did not rely on editing conventions such as direction matching to establish the spatial disposition of his characters, however; both Doyle and Rose enter the scene in one of the oblique long-shot framings grouping all the characters in a single shot. It is noteworthy that for the dénouement (Doyle tearing up the warrant), he brings the three remaining characters together in a medium long shot which is the longest take in the sequence by far (shot 54), so the different reactions to the situation and its resolution constitute a single picture as soon as possible.

Thus, the 1915 film version of *Alias Jimmy Valentine* can be seen to be constructed according to models from the tradition of situational dramaturgy in the theatre, even when it might seem, in the light of later filmmaking, at its most 'cinematic'. The point of the film is a situation; that situation is strung out to feature-film length, and the duration articulated by the concatenation of a series of lesser situations leading up to the central one; the staging of scenes is geared to the most effective presentation of situations, which means the production of a series of pictures; editing is not the presentation of a sequence of causally linked moments analysed out of the stream of the action which the viewer resynthesises into a coherent narrative, but a way to ensure that the pictorially organised situations are made visible to that viewer. The fact that Tourneur's film is the adaptation of a stage play makes it easier to demonstrate the situational logic at work in the story and its filmic presentation, but it should not be seen as defining it. The film is situational even when it presents an action such as the bank robbery, which is only implicit in the play. Rather, so many of the films of the 1910s, in America and Europe, are adaptations of stage plays because both live drama and films were conceived within the horizons of a situational dramaturgy. The development of cinematic devices in these years was not driven by a search for a uniquely cinematic aesthetic such as was championed by modernist filmmakers and critics in the 1920s, but by the specific means the film medium placed at the disposal of traditional situational ends.□

Notes

1. See Michael R. Booth, *Victorian Spectacular Theatre 1850–1910* (London: Routledge, 1981).

2. *Realisations: Narrative, Pictorial and Theatrical Arts in Nineteenth-Century England* (Princeton: Princeton University Press, 1983), esp. chapter 3: 'Speaking Pictures: The Drama', 38–51.

3. Ben Brewster and Lea Jacobs, *Theatre to Cinema: Stage Pictorialism and the Early Feature Film* (Oxford: Oxford University Press, 1997); see also Lea Jacobs, 'The Woman's Picture and the Poetics of Melodrama', *Camera Obscura* 31 (January–May 1993): 120–47.

4. For example, Peter Brooks's notion of the 'moral occult', explaining the prevalence of coincidence in nineteenth-century melodrama as a reassertion of the role of providence in reaction to the Enlightenment's rationalist critique of divine intervention in the world; see *The Melodramatic Imagination* (New Haven: Yale University Press, 1976).

5. *Uncle Tom's Cabin, or, Life among the Lowly* (New York: Samuel French, n.d. [1852]), 47. A similar scene, played with Eliza and Harry rather than Tom and Emmeline, possibly also with a tableau, appears in Act 2, scene 3 of Edward Fitzball's version, *Uncle Tom's Cabin, or, Negro Life in America* (London: John Dunscombe, n.d. [1852]).

6. Aristotle, *The Poetics* 6, 28 in Aristotle, *The Poetics*, Longinus, *On the Sublime*, and Demetrius, *On Style*, trans. W. Hamilton Fyfe and W. Rhys Roberts, Loeb Classical Library (Cambridge, Mass: Harvard University Press, 1927), 29; Gottfried Ephraim Lessing, *Laocoön: An Essay on the Limits of Painting and Poetry*, trans. Edward Allen McCormick (Baltimore: Johns Hopkins University Press, 1962), 19.

7. Preserved from an Australian nitrate print in the American Film Institute collection of the Library of Congress, the film is also available (transferred from the same copy), in the Library of Congress and Smithsonian video collection, no. 2: 'Origins of the Gangster Film'.

8. 'A Retrieved Reform', *The Cosmopolitan* 34, no. 6 (April 1903): 632–5. The title 'A Retrieved Reformation' is used in the subsequent anthologies that

included the story, starting with *Roads of Destiny* (New York: Doubleday, Page and Company, 1909), 161–72.

9. See *New York Dramatic Mirror* 53, no. 1620 (8 January 1910): 12; *ibid.* 53, no. 1623 (29 January 1910): 6; *The Theatre* 11, no. 108 (February 1910): 41; and *ibid.* 11, no. 109 (March 1910): supp. vii & x. There were 155 performances at Wallack's, a respectable, but by no means spectacular run (see Burns Mantle and Garrison P. Sherwood, ed., *The Best Plays of 1909–19, and the Year Book of the Drama in America* (New York: Dodd, Mead and Company, 1945), 411). A London production in March of 1910 starring Gerald du Maurier seems to have followed Armstrong's script; see *Illustrated London News* 136, no. 3703 (9 April 1910): 536; and *ibid.* 136, no. 3704 (16 April 1910): 568.

10. For extracts, see 'Music and Drama: "Alias Jimmy Valentine" – Paul Armstrong's Comedy of Roguedom,' *Current Literature* 49 (July 1910): 73–81; for novelisations, see *World Today* 18 (May 1910): 501–10 (by Lucy France Pierce), and *The Green Book Album* 4, no. 4 (October 1910): 705–29 (by Frank X. Finnegan).

11. The play was revived in 1921 with Otto Kruger in the lead. There is no indication what production any of the Billy Rose Library typescripts relates to.

12. See Edmond Stoullig, *Les Annales du théâtre et de la musique*, trentes eptième année, 1911 (Paris: Librairie Paul Ollendorff, 1912), 292. The play ran for 55 performances (*ibid.*, 301).

13. 'Movies Create Art', *Harper's Weekly* 62, no. 3097 (29 April 1916): 459.

14. Jean Mitry, 'Maurice Tourneur, 1876–1961', *Anthologie du cinéma*, vol. 4 (Paris: L'Avant-Scène & CIB, 1968), 268. The title role in *Le Mystérieux Jimmy* was played by Émile Chautard, who preceded Tourneur to Éclair's Paris studio and subsequently to the company's Fort Lee branch which became the Peerless Pictures studio where *Alias Jimmy Valentine* was made for World (by that time Chautard had returned to France). The name Maurice Tourneur does not appear in the cast as listed by Stoullig, op. cit., nor does Tourneur's real name, Maurice Thomas (he is listed as Tourneur in the casts of two other 1911 Théâtre de la Renaissance productions). The likelihood of Tourneur being entrusted with the direction is strengthened by the fact that neither Tarride himself nor any other well-known actor appeared in the play, and that it was an off-season production (Félix Duquesnel dismisses the acting in it as 'estivale' in *Le Théâtre* no. 302 (July 1911): 2).

15. See *Le Théâtre* no. 305 (September 1911): 20–23.

16. *La Escena Catalana* no. 296 (31 August 1929): 1–24.

17. Liebler was one of the theatrical impresarios who contributed films to the programme of features distributed by World film, which was dominated at the time by the Shubert brothers and William Brady. According to Kevin Lewis, the 1915 film version of *Alias Jimmy Valentine* was released as a Liebler production (see 'A World across from Broadway: The Shuberts and the Movies', *Film History* 1, no. 1 (1987): 42; and 'A World across from Broadway (II): Filmography of the World Film Corporation, 1913-22', *Film History* 1, no. 2 (1987): 168). There were two further American film versions – one in 1920 and another in 1929. In 1933, Lev Kuleshov used the story as a film within a film about O. Henry himself, *Velikii Uteshitel* (The Great Consoler). A sequel to *Alias Jimmy Valentine* was made in America in 1936 as *The Return of Jimmy Valentine* (with Robert Warwick in the lead again), and re-made in 1942 as *The Affairs of Jimmy Valentine*. A version of the original play was broadcast on American public television in 1986. See *The American Film Institute Catalog of Motion Pictures Produced in the United States*, volume F1: *Feature Films, 1911–1920*, ed. Patricia King Hanson and Alan Gevinson (Berkeley: University of California Press, 1988), entries F1.0046 and F1.0047; volume F2: *Feature Films, 1921–1930*, ed. Kenneth W. Munden (New York: R.R. Bowker, 1971), entry F2.0078; and volume F3: *Feature Films, 1931–1940*, ed. Hanson and Gevinson (Berkeley: University of California Press, 1993), entry F3.3704. The last entry has a detailed history of American film adaptations 1915 to 1986. For *Velikii Uteshitel*, see Jay Leyda, *Kino: A History of the Russian and Soviet Film* (London: Allen & Unwin, 1960), 438.

18. Though in the story (by contrast with the dramatisations), Jimmy is unaware of the detective's presence in Elmore until after he has opened the safe, and thus does not realise the full implications of the situation, unlike the reader.

19. But Kuleshov has two dénouements, the happy one in the framed story and a cynically unhappy one in the framing story.

20. 'Here is something new in climaxes which makes the "practical" buzzsaw and the "real" waterfall go away back and sit down,' cited from *The World* in an advertisement in an unattributed clipping in the *Alias Jimmy Valentine* Theater File in the Museum of the City of New York; 'One of the tensest situations imaginable', *New York Dramatic Mirror* 53, no. 1623 (29 January 1910): 6; 'The big situation of the play', *Illustrated London News* 136, no. 3703

(9 April 1910): 536; 'a "coup de théâtre"', *Le Théâtre* (September 1911): 22.

21. *Op. cit.* Tourneur goes on to claim that, by contrast, there is little difference between Armstrong's play and his film version of it.

22. This is not so much stated as assumed by guides to play writing, which discuss where in a story the play should start, but present all the action, as opposed to events referred to in dialogue, as proceeding in temporal order thereafter. The prescription is explicit in screen writing manuals: 'The scene that happens Friday must be shown before the scene that happens on Saturday and you must show what happened at nine o'clock before that which happens at half past ten. If you do not you will get your audience so badly mixed up that they will lose interest in the plot and vote the play tiresome' (Epes Winthrop Sargent, *Technique of the Photoplay*, 2nd ed. (New York: The Moving Picture World, 1913), 38). There were exceptions to the rule, the most famous of which (in drama) is *The Corsican Brothers*, whose first act ends with one brother at home in Corsica having a vision of the other's death in a duel in Paris; the second act relates the events that lead up to a second representation of the duel. Elmer Rice's *On Trial* (1914) is usually taken as the first important American play to use flashbacks to tell its story. There was something of a vogue for stories built (like *On Trial*'s) around flashbacks in both European and American short films in the early 1910s, but features largely avoided such construction. See Ben Brewster, '*Traffic in Souls*: An Experiment in Feature-Length Narrative Construction', *Cinema Journal* 31, no. 1 (Fall 1991): 48–9.

23. *A Retrieved Reformation*, it should be said, avoids manipulating the time sequence to tell its backstory. It conveys Jimmy's character as a hardened professional criminal by what Barthes calls an index ('Introduction to the Structural Analysis of Narratives' in *Image-Music-Text*, ed. and trans. Stephen Heath (London: Fontana/Collins, 1977), 92), when Jimmy, on his release, rescues from a secret hiding place his suitcase of special made-to-order burglar's tools, and by the narration of a memory, when the discovery of a collar stud on his bedroom floor reminds him of the struggle when he was arrested. (This collar stud is presumably the germ of the cuff-link that Doyle finds on the floor in the bank and which leads him to Valentine in the film version.)

24. 'Mr Warner's portrayal is notable in its artistic sincerity', 'The Players', *Everybody's Magazine* 72, no. 5 (May 1910): 703; 'Mr Warner plays with reserve and sincerity', *The Sun*, cited from an advertisement in an unattributed clipping in the *Alias*

Jimmy Valentine Theater File in the Museum of the City of New York.

25. 'Unlike the average detective story, it does not tend to idealise or romanticise hopelessly vicious and depraved characters', *The Theatre* 11, no. 108 (February 1910): 41; see also an unattributed review by Alan Dale in a clipping in a scrapbook in the Daniel Blum collection of the Wisconsin Center for Film and Theater Research, microfilm 961 reel 4 frame 854: '*Alias Jimmy Valentine* is not in the same class as our old friends Raffles, Jim the Penman, and Arsène Lupin [... It] will not be discussed as a glorification of crime.'

26. Hassan El Nouty, *Théâtre et pré-cinéma: Essai sur la problématique du spectacle au XIXe siècle* (Paris: A.G. Nizet, 1978), 87; El Nouty's example is the set prescribed for the first act of *La Reine Margot*, by Alexandre Dumas *père* (1847), representing rooms on two floors of La Hurière's inn and the streets outside. English examples go back at least to Edward Fitzball's *Jonathan Bradford, or, The Murder at the Roadside Inn* of 1833. See M. St. Clare Byrne, 'Early Multiple Settings in England', *Theatre Notebook* 8 (1954): 81–6; and Peter Winn, 'Multiple Settings on the Early Nineteenth-Century London Stage', *Theatre Notebook* 35 (1981): 17–24.

27. See Kevin Brownlow, 'Ben Carré', *Sight and Sound* 49, no. 1 (Winter 1979–80): 46–50, especially the illustration on 49.

28. In fact, there is another scene which might be so named in both the plays and the film, the one in which Jimmy and Red deliberately leave Avery alone in Jimmy's office in the bank at Springfield, Illinois, with a tray of banknotes. In the French and Catalan version (where the temptation is suffered by Dick le Rat/el Rata), the scene becomes the mystery climax of Act 2. In the American play, the incident presents a comic variation on the theme of the criminal's conversion. I will not deal with it, however, as the resolution of the situation of suspense (Avery's discovery that he cannot bear to betray his comrades by stealing the money they have entrusted to him) is missing from the surviving print of the film.

29. See an unattributed clipping in the *Alias Jimmy Valentine* Theater File in the Museum of the City of New York, and *Cosmopolitan* 48, no. 6 (May 1910): 755.

30. In the print there is a direct cut between the last two vision scenes, with no fades, and no intervening return to scene. I assume this is the result of missing footage, and there would have been both fades and another variant of the shot of the three remembering characters in the film as released.

31. A similar gesture appears in an illustratation to Montcornet's review of *Le Mystérieux Jimmy* in *Le Théâtre* 305 (September 1911): 21, captioned 'Act II'; the only plausible point in Act 2 in *El misteriós Jimmy Samson* for such a gesture is when the third member of the trio of ex-criminals to arrive in Springfield (here Dick el Rata) agrees to go straight: 'DICK: Em quedo el costat teu: seré un home honrat: serem tres homes honrats. AVERY: M'ho esperava. SAMSON: (A en Dick, donant-li les mans) Ja veuràs, Dick, quina calma, quin repòs, quin benestar més dolç s'hi troba dintre aquesta vida!' (*La Escena Catalana* 296 (31 August 1929): 15). Although the direction only indicates that Jimmy takes Dick's hands, in the French version, at least, all three seem to have joined hands, which Dick's reference to 'three honest men' would make appropriate to the Catalan version, too. The occurrence of this gesture at exactly the same point in the French play and the film again suggests the influence of the former on the latter.

32. This is not certain, since the film only survives as fragments deposited at the Copyright Office, and these do not include the ends of any of the scenes.

33. Because the sequence is linked to its predecessor by an alternation, it would be hard to be precise about the number, even if one were confident that the film is still in its original release form. The figure 58 includes titles and inserts, and takes as its starting point the shot in which Red and Jimmy arrive by the safe in the vault. However, jump cuts and strong ellipses at the beginning suggest footage is missing there, as well as at the end, which has been restored in the video version with a freeze frame and fade out where one would expect at least a closing reconciliation between Valentine and Rose – perhaps in the same shot, perhaps with more than one shot. As is common with surviving prints from this period, subsequent re-editing for re-release or by collectors may have increased the number of shots to approximate later cutting rates. Allowing for all these vicissitudes, however, there can be no doubt that there were a fairly large number of shots in the scene as first released.

34. See the scrapbooks of the Daniel Blum Collection of the Wisconsin Center for Film and Theater Research, vol. 28 (1909–10), microfilm 961 reel 4 frame 854.

35. 'The Plays of the Week', *New York Dramatic Mirror* 63, no. 1623 (29 January 1910): 6.

36. It is worth noting that, his reputation as a 'painterly' director notwithstanding, Tourneur rarely resorts to lighting effects in his films of the 1910s. When *Alias Jimmy Valentine* was made, Cecil B. DeMille's cameraman, Alvin Wyckoff, was already using the chiaroscuro or so-called 'Rembrandt' lighting for which Lasky films of the 1910s are still famous. For an account of how these lighting effects were inspired by David Belasco's stage lighting but employed means appropriate only to filmmaking, see Lea Jacobs, 'Belasco, DeMille and the Development of Lasky Lighting', *Film History* 5, no. 4 (December 1993): 405–18.

37. See for example *The Green Book Album* 4, no. 4 (October 1910): facing 705; *Hampton's Magazine* 24 (May 1910): 701; *Harper's Weekly* 54, no. 2776 (5 March 1910): 24.

38. See *Julius Cahn's Official Theatrical Guide, Containing Information of the Leading Theaters and Attractions in America* (New York: Publication Office, Empire Theater), vol. 9 (1904–5): 43 and 158.

39. F.H. Richardson recommended a screen width of 12 feet in 1910 ('Operator's Column', *Moving Picture World* 7, no. 9 (27 August 1910): 470); John Klaber 12 feet in 1915 ('Planning the Moving Picture Theatre', *Architectural Record* 38, no. 5 (November 1915): 540); the same year in Britain, Colin Bennett recommended 10 to 12 feet for a throw of 45 feet, and 15 to 19 for one of 80 feet ('Knotty Points Answered', *Kinematograph and Lantern Weekly* 20, no. 447 (18 November 1915): 71); in 1917 Edward Kinsila proposed a 12-foot screen for a 50-foot throw, and a 15-foot one for a 75-foot throw (*Modern Theatre Construction* (New York: Chalmers, 1917), 106).

40. Such strained plausibility is found in films at this period, notably in the scene in which Count Spinelli is hidden in the van Houvens' drawing-room in Benjamin Christensen's *Det hemmelighedsfulde X* (Denmark, 1914), remaining for long periods concealed only by a chimney embrasure two feet away from characters who are supposed to be unaware of his presence.

Film History, Volume 9, pp. 410–434, 1997. Copyright © John Libbey & Company
ISSN: 0892-2160. Printed in Australia

Narration early in the transition to classical filmmaking: Three Vitagraph shorts

Kristin Thompson

his essay follows up on some ideas concerning early classical film narration laid out in my portions of *The Classical Hollywood Cinema*.[1] There I suggested that the primitive and classical cinemas were two distinct approaches to filmmaking, and that the classical cinema did not simply evolve out of the earlier type, but resulted from fundamental changes in formal and functional strategies, on the levels of both style and narrative. We may usefully consider the primitive cinema to have been dominant up to about 1908, and the classical system of filmmaking to have been fully formulated by 1917. The period from approximately 1909 to 1916 involved a transition between the two approaches. During those years, devices and functions from the primitive period continued to exist alongside newer classical strategies – often within the same film.

I have suggested that one could distinguish the primitive and classical systems of filmmaking partly on the basis of their radically different conceptions of narration, defined here as the set of all devices by which a film conveys narrative information, cueing the spectator to comprehend actively the ongoing cause and effect relationships and to form hypotheses about probable upcoming events.[2] My original description of the difference between primitive and classical narration was:

During the primitive period, the narration usually remained omniscient, with action placed in a block before the viewer – played out in a long-shot view for the most part. (Even dreams, visions, and memories were seen in superimposition over only part of the shot, thus minimising the subjective effect and keeping the narration omniscient.) As [André] Gaudreault suggests, 'The narrator was not *conscious* of being a narrator'. Intertitles of neutral, non-self-conscious tone summarised action and introduced characters. But the narration seldom attempted to guide the spectator actively. The rare early cut-ins or camera movements which occurred stand out in this context as moments of more self-conscious narration aimed at shaping the onlooker's perception. (Later, when such moments became part of the norm, they would call less attention to the process of narration, with continuity principles foregrounding narrative flow and making cutting unobtrusive.) In short, classical narration

Kristin Thompson's latest book is *Film History: An Introduction* (with David Bordwell). Please address correspondence to 2914 Irvington Way, Madison WI 53713, USA. Fax (608) 271-8547.

tailored every detail to the spectator's attention; the primitive cinema's narration had done so only sporadically.[3]

It may be useful to examine these distinctions in greater detail, using films from the early transitional period, when films were drawing upon narrational strategies of both primitive and classical filmmaking.

I have chosen to examine the narration in three one-reelers made by the Vitagraph company in the early 1910s: *The Inherited Taint* (1911), *At the Eleventh Hour* (1912) and *The Tiger* (1913). These titles were chosen from the list of viewing prints of Vitagraph films available at the National Archive in London, on the basis of their dates; subject matter, style, and quality were not considered in the selection, since the films were not viewed before making the choices. This process fortuitously turned up three films whose narrational strategies were quite distinct from one another. The films also show a distinct progression from a heavy dependence on narrational devices common in the primitive film (*The Inherited Taint*), to devices completely typical of the early transitional period (*At the Eleventh Hour*), to devices which strongly suggest classical principles at work (*The Tiger*).

I do not wish, however, to suggest that all films made in 1911 to 1913 would display this clear-cut progression. Films using a variety of strategies were being made at the same time, and there was no smooth progress toward a purely classical system. *At the Eleventh Hour* resembles many films from both 1911 and 1912 and seems completely typical, while *The Inherited Taint* is a bit old-fashioned for 1911 (especially when one considers that it was released at about the same time as Griffith's *The Lonedale Operator*); *The Tiger*, at least in its decoupage in two lengthy sequences, draws upon continuity principles in a more sophisticated way than would most films of 1913.

Vitagraph is generally held by historians to have been one of the most innovative of the early American studios. The main reason for this was its consistent use of the 'nine-foot line' beginning in 1909; such a staging placed the actors closer to the camera than was common, with the lower frame line cutting them off at about the knee or slightly below. Barry Salt also attributes innovations in

lower camera heights to the Vitagraph company during the period 1909 to 1912.[4] By the early 1910s, however, closer framings and slightly lower camera heights had become conventional in other studios as well, and I think we can take many Vitagraph films of this period to be largely typical of what was going on across the industry. Certainly neither *The Inherited Taint* nor *At the Eleventh Hour* is outstanding or atypical; *The Tiger* is a flashier film, but as a whole, the three would seem to represent a fair cross-section of the early transitional period.

In examining the narration in these three films, I shall be drawing upon descriptive categories discussed in David Bordwell's *Narration in the Fiction Film*.[5] There he suggests that a film's narration can be characterised primarily by its degrees of knowledge, self-consciousness, and communicativeness. That is, the narration can know a great deal about narrative events that take place in different times and places and that involve all the characters; in this case we assume it to be omniscient. A film which cuts freely among events and which reveals more than any one character or group would know has a highly knowledgeable narration. One common means by which the narration's knowledge is restricted is through sticking close to one character or group which can only have limited access to the narrative's overall events.

Narration can be more or less self-conscious, in that it can draw attention to the act of giving information, or it can make that information seem to come straight out of the action with no mediating devices. For example, a dialogue title would usually be a case of relatively unself-conscious narration, since the information comes to us from the characters in the scene. An expository title of a completely neutral tone might be slightly more self-conscious, while an expository title that adopted an ironic tone and used elaborate poetic language would be more self-conscious yet. I should emphasise, however, that narrational self-consciousness is a matter of historical norms. A device that conforms closely to usage in its period will tend to be less self-conscious than an innovative or atypical one. Hence a dialogue title in 1905, when such titles were virtually unknown, would presumably appear more self-conscious than any type of expository title could. Similarly, in the late 1910s, intertitles with an ironic tone were far more common than they had been in the early 1910s, and hence a narration which drew upon them was proportionally less self-conscious. Similarly, a track forward to reveal a detail would be less self-conscious as a device in the 1940s than in the 1920s.

Finally, a film's narration will be more or less communicative. It may have a certain range of knowledge but choose to suppress it. For example, early 1910 films were heavily dependent upon written material within the space of the action – letters, telegrams, signed photographs, and the like – shown in close views, called inserts. If a film shows us a series of inserts of this type, then shows a character reading a letter and fails to show us an insert, the narration is being uncommunicative. It presumably could show us the writing, but does not.

Bordwell has characterised the classical Hollywood cinema using these concepts:

> Very generally, we can say that classical narration tends to be omniscient, highly communicative, and only moderately self-conscious. That is, the narration knows more than all the characters, conceals relatively little (chiefly 'what will happen next'), and seldom acknowledges its own address to the audience.[6]

A given film, however, will not necessarily employ narration that is completely fixed in its use of the three strategies. It need not have fixed degrees of knowledge and self-consciousness and communicativeness throughout but may fluctuate as it goes along. Genre conventions can motivate departures from the classical norm described in the above passage. Any type of film that depends on suspense, for example, will tend to be less communicative than a musical, say, or a comedy. Moreover, the properties of the narration will often fluctuate systematically across the film; the beginnings and endings, both of whole films and of individual scenes, will often be the most self-conscious, omniscient, and communicative.[7]

Using these categories, then, how can we further specify the differences between primitive and classical narrational systems? I suggested above that the primitive cinema placed the action 'in a block' before the viewer. That is, the narration would stage a shot's action as a unit to be presented to the spectator with relatively little guidance to help

him or her sort out the phases of the action, the more important characters from the incidental ones, and so on. The staging often centered the key actions, but simultaneous actions occurring in equally prominent parts of the screen were common. When several actors are present, they were likely to be lined up across the frame, their expressions and gestures competing for our attention. Cut-ins and camera movements were relatively rare, and hence small gestures and objects were often difficult to see.

Methods varied between interiors and exteriors. Interiors were usually aimed toward a centered, fixed spectator at a distance from the action, seeing it straight-on; it was as if the spectator were situated at the top of an isosceles triangle, with the backdrop the triangle's base. All action would then be organised around that frontal, fixed view. Such organisation ensured that the spectator would be able to see most of what happened on the screen, but not necessarily that he or she would be able to see it clearly. Interiors also placed the spectator at a distance, and the actors seldom approached the camera close enough for their feet to be cut off by the lower frame line. (As we have seen, the *plan americain* began to be normalised in 1909.) This neutral gap in the foreground emphasised the sense that the action was being organised to be displayed to a spectator in a fixed spot in front of the playing space.

Exteriors took quite a different approach, but still, I think, presented blocks of action to the spectator. True, many exteriors involved chases or other situations where the characters moved swiftly from the depth of the scene and passed very close to the camera in exiting. Here again, however, the spectator is at a distance from the action for most of the shot's duration, and the action is organised around the direction of that fixed vantage-point. That is, the actors do not run directly toward the spectator/camera, but they run forward from depth at a diagonal that is at an acute angle to the spectator's point of view and is calculated to keep them in view for a long time. I would argue that the organisation in depth was done in exteriors, as in interiors, primarily to keep the entire action visible to the spectator without the necessity to shift vantage-points during the action's span. In the chase, in other words, the 'block' of action is primarily temporal. Were chases staged from side to side within the scene, with the spectator watching from a point perpendicular to the runner's trajectory, the actors would appear only at intervals in the shot: the pursued would run quickly through, with a gap ensuing before the first pursuers' entrance and another before that of the inevitable stragglers. Note that in primitive chase films, virtually all shots begin with the pursued entering from off screen and hold until the last chaser exits before the cut to the next shot comes. Despite the greater depth and the lack of a neutral space between the camera and the space of the action, exteriors also usually present a self-contained unit of action, uninterrupted by additional narrational cues. The major narrational cues for both interiors and exteriors, then, were centered around acting, decor, staging, framing, and occasional written material in the form of intertitles and inserts.

The result is a highly knowledgeable kind of narration. Primitive films seldom suggest that the narration is limited to one character's range or knowledge or that the narration is unreliable. In *The Life of an American Fireman* (Edison, 1903), for example, the narration anticipates that the fire alarm will be rung and it cuts to a view of the alarm just before the hand comes into the frame. The same holds true for chase scenes, in which the narration usually takes us to the spot where the next action will occur before the characters themselves arrive there.

Primitive narration is for the most part unselfconscious as well. As Gaudreault put it in the passage quoted above: 'The narrator was not *conscious* of being an narrator.' Because the action is displayed to the viewer in units, with few additional cues to guide perception, the narration remains for the most part neutral and unobtrusive. The few intertitles are usually straightforward summaries of the action to come or, very rarely, dialogue titles. Looking back at the primitive period from a modern perspective, when classical-style narration has long been established as the norm, it is easy to assume that the various 'strange' story-telling conventions do constitute a self-conscious approach to narration. But it seems more likely that in the preclassical cinema, narration did not systematically call attention to itself. For example, some primitive films use a set construction where two rooms are visible side by side, with a wall separating them. In *A Policeman's Love Affair* (Lubin, 1904), such a set

allows the spectator to see simultaneous action in two rooms. *Foul Play* (Vitagraph, 1907) shows a woman spying on a man through a keyhole; the wall between the hallway and the room beyond is built just wide enough to contain the door itself, with the room beyond clearly visible.[8] A filmmaker confronted with the narrational problem of showing simultaneous actions in adjoining rooms might have a number of stylistic options available at any given time, and the one she or he takes depends partly upon the period's stylistic norms. A transitional or classical film would be likely to cut between the two rooms (e.g. *The Lonely Villa*, American Biograph, 1909). But such an option was far less likely in 1904 and 1907. Some films might opt for a keyhole-masked point-of-view shot (e.g. *A Search for Evidence*, American Mutoscope & Biograph, 1903). The option of using a cutaway set was probably as common, or even more so, than cutting between two rooms. Hence, although a cutaway set may today seem a self-conscious device, it probably was not intended or taken as such during this early period.

All this is not to suggest that self-conscious narration did not exist in any primitive films. Many films contained comic or allegorical touches imposed upon the action by an overarching commentary. Edwin S. Porter's *The Kleptomaniac* (Edison, 1905) makes an overt comment through the use of intertitles and a symbolic, non-diegetic image of a statue of Justice. The common use of close views to begin and end films (a fashion apparently started in 1903 by Porter's *The Great Train Robbery*) added a bit of narrational commentary; for example, *The 100-to-One Shot*'s (Vitagraph, 1906) opening shot of a hand clutching money, or the *Bold Bank Robbery*'s (Lubin, 1904) 'before and after' shots of the three thieves that open and close the film. It seems that, as in the classical period, such self-conscious narration in primitive films tends to come at the beginnings and endings of the narrative. (In a film like *The Whole Dam Family and the Dam Dog* (Edison, 1905), the comic close views of the various family members and the animated title card take up the bulk of the footage – to the point where this film can hardly be said to contain a narrative as such.)

The degree of the primitive cinema's communicativeness is difficult to determine. On the one hand, primitive films often fail to emphasise important events and relationships, leaving the spectator to notice them on his or her own. On the other hand, such films seldom deliberately withhold such information. The action appears on the screen, for those to see who can. Many primitive films, as Charles Musser has pointed out, stick to familiar narratives so that even should small-scale unclarities arise, the audience would arrive having a general knowledge of the narrative's outlines.[9] The frequent experiments with new narrational means also suggests a desire on the part of filmmakers to present narrative information more clearly. Yet primitive narration on the whole lacks the redundancy and the break-down of the action into a linear chain of causes and effects that make the classical narrative so easy to follow. Perhaps we can say that primitive narration was moderately communicative.

These principles of redundancy and clarity guided the formulation of a classical approach to narration. The classical cinema, in comparison with the primitive, developed a systematically wider range within each of these areas. A classical film might be omniscient, but it could occasionally limit its narration's knowledge. The classical cinema's systematic use of occasional self-conscious devices, however, clearly made narration more flexible. Similarly, classical narration's communicativeness might in general be greater than that of the primitive cinema, but a set of conventions for withholding information also came into use. These might have to do with suspense, or a film might use character psychology to reveal events gradually.

In looking at the three transitional Vitagraph films, then, we can expect to see a growing emphasis on redundancy and linear cause–effect action, as well as a development in the range of types of narration being systematically used. This is not to imply that the move into a classical approach represented progress and that the new methods were better than those used in the primitive era – only that major differences existed, and that these crucially involved techniques of narration.

The Inherited Taint

If we can assume that the transitional cinema of the early 1910s involved a mixture of devices and functions from both the primitive and classical modes, then *The Inherited Taint* remains closer to the primitive period. It avoids narrational aids like

---

The Inherited Taint (released 31 March 1911)
Cast: Maurice Costello (Herbert Waring),
Lillian Walker (Pearl), Helen Gardner
(Kathleen Holt)

℘ ℘ ℘

Herbert Waring receives his inheritance and a letter from his late guardian, warning him to avoid 'the Curse of Drink', which ruined his father. At a birthday supper, Herbert declines to join in a toast. A month later, just after his engagement to Pearl Langdon has been announced, Herbert finds her in the arms of a rival and breaks with her; this disappointment leads him to drink heavily, and he is sent to a sanatorium. There he falls in love with a sympathetic nurse. Upon his discharge from the sanatorium, he declares his love, but she says only if he can stay sober for a year will she consent to marry him. At a party, he meets Pearl again, and she successfully tempts him to drink. Back home, however, a photograph of the nurse inspires him to sober up, and he returns to claim her hand.

---

shot/reverse shots, cut-ins, or dialogue intertitles, even though all three were in occasional use by 1911. For the most part, the films depends upon very conventionalised situations, characters, and events, which the spectator will usually not even have to figure out – he/she simply recognises them from previous experience with other narratives.[10] In those scenes where actions occur which are too complex to be conveyed in pantomime, or where objects too small to be seen in long-shot framing are introduced, the action remains unclear. As a result, *The Inherited Taint* deals primarily with extremely obvious causal action, with an occasional obscure passage. Its narration, by failing to help us understand such moments, remains uncommunicative by the standards of the classical cinema – and, to a slight extent, even by standards of the 1911 period.

The opening exposition is clear enough. The title, *The Inherited Taint*, already suggests a vice, most likely a fondness for alcohol. The first expository title (ET) repeats 'The inherited taint', followed immediately by a second, 'Herbert Waring receives his inheritance and a letter'. So far the narration is wholly knowledgeable and largely communicative. We know the hero's name and suspect his problem (even though the 'taint' is not specified). The upper-middle-class living room of the opening scene sets the milieu of the action, and the older man giving the papers to the younger one is clearly a lawyer (the mention of an inheritance plus the man's brief-case and pince-nez); the younger man is thus our hero, Herbert.

The lawyer's reluctance to hand over the letter and his worried reaction at the end of the scene further suggest a threat, and this is confirmed in the next scene. The opening ET, 'A dangerous inheritance', repeats the idea of an anticipated danger, though the title again fails to specify the problem. The letter which Herbert reads, and which we see in an insert, confirms our suspicions: Herbert's father was ruined by drink, and Herbert's late guardian warns him not to succumb to this inherited taint.

So far, the presentation of information has been straightforward. All the action has been centered in the shots (with a reframing movement to aid this process when Herbert sits down to read the letter); no important actions have competed within the same shot for our attention; the titles and insert have spelled everything out.

The next scene varies this slightly. After a summary title, 'A birthday supper. A warning heeded', we see a formal dinner party, with several tables in a large room. There has been an effort to create a realistically deep staging here, with most of the diners having their backs to us or their faces largely concealed by the foreground diners (Fig. 1). Such arrangements of characters were coming into occasional use during 1911. The staging situates Herbert to the far right of the frame, but even though he is not central, the narration singles him out, for he is the only one in profile and the only one whose face is clearly visible. His placement at the head of the table is confusingly motivated, as the title does not tell whether or not this is *his* birthday (another bit of uncommunicativeness). We will probably assume that it is. At any rate, he is an honoured guest, since he rises to give a speech and propose a toast, before remembering the warning and lowering his glass without drinking.

The next two scenes follow the course of Herbert's romance with, as the first ET describes her,

Fig. 1. *The Inherited Taint*

'The belle of the season, with two strings to her bow'. A long shot of a sitting room follows, with the woman receiving a visit from Herbert's rival, who hides when Herbert arrives to take her out. Here and through most of the film the action is laid out in an extremely linear fashion. Other narrational possibilities that existed at this time are ignored, but we shall see them at work in the other two films: multiple actions and depth within the shot in *At the Eleventh Hour* and decoupage to break the action into units, in *The Tiger*.

Another title informs us: 'One month later. An engagement announced.' This summary indicates the rather arbitrary nature of the narration's communicativeness. On the one hand, it tells us how much time has passed. The time lapse is of minimal causal importance here, yet later on in the film, when the passage of time becomes more important, the narration fails to inform us about it. In fact, although the film seems to cover a lengthy stretch of time, apparently a bit more than a year, we get no very clear sense of temporal relations among most scenes. This ET does not specify whose engagement is being announced; given the action of the previous scene, Pearl might have become engaged to either Herbert or his rival. The suspense as to which it is continues as Herbert enters with Pearl; they kiss and he leaves. A confusing bit of by-play then goes on, as she picks up a small object which he has left behind, starts to run after him, then shrugs and comes back to the foreground, carrying it. As she hears the rival approaching, she hides the object. Given its tiny size, we are unable to see what this

Fig. 2. *The Inherited Taint*

Fig. 3. *The Inherited Taint*

Fig. 4. *The Inherited Taint*

shouts at Pearl, picks up the small object (which, it now at last becomes clear, must be a ring case), and stalks out. Pearl cries, but the rival consoles her, and she quickly laughs and kisses him.

Throughout the film, the narration has remained omniscient. We know more than Herbert does, as when we notice the lawyer's worried expression in the first scene or discern Pearl's duplicity as soon as she is introduced. Yet we never find out what her motives are – why she gets engaged to Herbert when she has no intention of marrying him, and later why she tries to lure Herbert back into drinking. She is clearly in the plot primarily to be the cause of his drinking and his later near-relapse, but the narration fails to motivate her behaviour (as it could easily do in a brief title identifying her as a golddigger or a mischiefmaker or whatever).

At any rate, Pearl's initial function being accomplished, another expository intertitle repeats the phrase, 'the inherited taint', and we see the beginning of Herbert's anticipated decline. Here again an omniscient narration creates an absolutely comprehensible scene. The initial framing places Herbert in the middle ground as he orders the old family retainer to bring in something to drink (Fig. 2). The butler looks upset, but goes out the door at the left on his errand. From the start, the prominently placed chair and table in the foreground have suggested that a major action will occur there, and Herbert now moves forward and sits. This movement places him low in the frame, but the servant immediately returns with a tray, thereby taking up the top portion

object is, and the action does not make it easy to identify its nature. Is it an engagement ring in a case? (But if so, and she is engaged to Herbert, why would she try to return it?) A cut-in or a title might have cleared this up, but none is used. There is no apparent reason, either, why the film should withhold such information.

The rival's entrance leads to the confirmation that Herbert is now engaged to Pearl. He angrily shows her a newspaper announcement (seen in an insert). She assures him, in mime, that she really does not love Herbert, and they embrace. A summary title, 'An engagement broken', leads to Herbert's return; upon seeing the pair embracing, he

Fig. 5. *The Inherited Taint*

Fig. 6. *The Inherited Taint*

of the composition (Fig. 3). After some business in which the servant gestures anxiously again, he exits, this time for good. A reframe down (Fig. 4) primes us to expect that he will not return and that Herbert is about to succumb to the taint in a drinking bout (which he confirms by becoming drunk immediately after beginning his imbibition).

The next scene begins with the title, 'The downward path'. A row of bottles on the bookshelf at the left also signals the change; it had not been there in the previous scene. When one of the men playing cards at the centre table tries to stop the already inebriated Herbert from getting another drink, a struggle breaks out (Fig. 5). At the entrance of Herbert's lawyer, however, the group breaks up and moves to the sides of the frame, allowing us a clear view of the newcomer (Fig. 6). The staging here is somewhat awkward but clearly designed in order to allow the spectator to see what is going on. (In 1911, the option of cutting in to a character entering at the rear of a scene was a highly unlikely one.) Herbert's collapse and the departure of the guests end this scene.

The next, brief scene, introduced by the title, 'The doctor', serves simply to get Herbert sent to 'The sanitorium', as the subsequent scene is labelled by *its* opening title. Indeed, the bulk of the film's titles do not summarise the upcoming action in any detail. Rather, as in these cases, they simply label it: 'The downward path', 'The doctor', 'The sanitorium'. The narration is able to use such phrases because the situations are so conventional – the titles, in

effect, simply refer to the conventions. There is no need for the film to specify, 'Herbert is forced to go into a sanitorium', since we have been suspecting that something of this sort will happen. The intertitles will continue to appeal to convention in order to aid the spectator in understanding the action up to the end of the film: 'In the world again', 'Tempted' and 'Love Conquers'. The result is certainly a clear narrative, but one that cannot risk complexity or innovation without creating spectator confusion.

The sanitorium scene demonstrates how dependent the film's narration is upon pantomime, never using dialogue titles (DT). This lengthy shot stands for Herbert's entire recovery period and for his growing love for his nurse, so it must convey a considerable amount of information – yet there is neither a summary of the action at the beginning nor a DT once the nurse enters. We see Herbert staring sadly out the window at the beginning, then talking earnestly with the nurse after her entrance. Yet we never learn whether this is his first moment of attraction to her or they have some sort of ongoing relationship. She speaks earnestly to him, but is this merely a pep-talk? Has he been at the sanitorium for some time and is now declaring his love? Is this taking place near the beginning of his stay? Similarly, in the next scene (introduced as 'Herbert leaves the sanitorium'), the action is all conveyed in pantomime. The nurse enters Herbert's room and seems disappointed that no one is present; presumably she thinks he has gone without saying goodbye. When he enters, an elaborate bit of mime

Fig. 7. *The Inherited Taint*

Fig. 8. *The Inherited Taint*

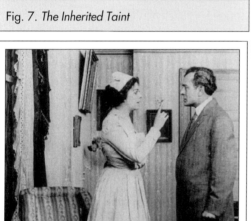

Fig. 9. *The Inherited Taint*

Fig. 10. *The Inherited Taint*

conveys the essentials of the action, but it cannot specify all the details which a DT could easily convey. He begins by apparently declaring his love for her, and probably asking her to marry him, by using a conventional hand-to-heart gesture (Fig. 7). She responds with several gestures – pointing to the door (Fig. 8), holding up one finger (Fig. 9), and clasping her hands together (Fig. 10), while Herbert reacts by looking disappointed. Presumably she has told him something like, 'Go out into the world, stay sober for a year, and then I'll marry you'.[11] After this he responds (judging by his lip movements, he says 'I promise') and leaves with his lawyer.

The scene ('In the world again') of the party at which Herbert meets Pearl again and succumbs to the temptation to drink is remarkable as the only one in the whole film where there are two different framings not connected by a reframing camera movement. We see Pearl and the rival in a conservatory just off a ballroom. The rival leaves, and Herbert enters; Pearl recognises and greets him (Fig. 11). A title, 'Tempted', provides a transition to a longer view of this same action but now with a new foreground space revealed (Fig. 12). For the first and only time, the narration uses a cut (albeit one covered by an intertitle) to bring in a new, causally salient element – a table, laden with champagne and punch, at the left foreground of the shot. Again, the narration anticipates the temporal trajectory of this new shot by placing a chair prominently in the

Fig. 11. *The Inherited Taint*

Fig. 12. *The Inherited Taint*

foreground; the couple moves forward into *plan americain*, and Pearl sits in the chair. Her pantomime seems to suggest that she regrets her past behaviour toward Herbert (though we saw at the beginning of the scene that she is still romantically linked to the rival). She asks for a drink and urges him to have one with her. As in her earlier scene, we have no indication as to why she is doing this. It may be for revenge, since when he becomes (as before) instantly drunk and tries to embrace her, she draws away and laughs. He takes another glass of wine, then leaves.

The next intertitle assures us that all will end well: 'Love conquers.' Back at home, Herbert orders the servant to bring something to drink. He leans on the bookshelf, not noticing – as we do – that the nurse's photograph is prominently displayed there. As he is about to drink, however, he sees it and picks it up, looking first at the glass, then at the photo (Fig. 13). The choice between the two is made quite explicit; he smashes the glass to the floor and kisses the portrait. A final intertitle, 'Herbert receives his reward', leads to the reunion between the two in his former room at the sanitorium. Here the narration could have made things clearer by specifying that the his one year of required sobriety has passed. As it is, we are left with only a vague sense of the passing of the temporal injunction she had laid upon him.

Overall, the narration of *The Inherited Taint* depends upon four main cues: staging, largely static framing (with reframings, but no other types

of camera movement), pantomimic acting, and written material (intertitles and inserts). Editing functions almost entirely to link separate scenes, rather than to convey information. The action is very simple and conventional in most cases, and where it is unclear, there is seldom an attempt to provide the audience with additional narrational cues. Our remaining two films will demonstrate some other tactics used to signal more complex narrative information to the viewer.

At the Eleventh Hour

The opening scene of the film needs to convey several important bits of narrative information quickly, and its does so through a combination of summary ETs and rapid pantomime on the parts of the four principal actors. The opening title, 'Richards refuses $5,000 for his railroad bonds', leads into a *plan americain* where the two men, Daley and Richards, stand at the left foreground, while their wives chat in the background right. We learn which of the two men is Richards when the man on the right pulls out the bonds and shows them to the other; both men are smiling. After only a few seconds another title appears: 'Mrs Daley shows her new diamond necklace.' A return to the same framing shows Richards with his hand in his pocket (where he has presumably replaced the bonds 'during' the title), and Daley, no longer smiling, stares at him with a concerned expression (Fig. 14). Simultaneously, in the background, Mrs Daley is in the process of being

Fig. 13. *The Inherited Taint*

Fig. 14. *At the Eleventh Hour*

At the Eleventh Hour (released 6 August 1912)
Director: William V. Ranous.
Scenario: Charles S. Gaskill
Cast: Herbert L. Barry (Mr Richards),
Zena Kiefe (His Wife), Harry Northrup
(Mr Daley), Lillian Walker (His Wife)

℘ ℘ ℘

Mr Richards refuses a $5,000 offer from Mr Daley for his railroad bonds. A necklace is delivered to Mrs Daley, who shows it to her husband and Mr and Mrs Richards. Later, when Mrs Richards is invited to a reception, she borrows the new necklace. As the Richards are leaving the party, a thief steals the necklace. Mr Richards is upset, but gives in to his wife's plea that he replace it; he buys a $12,000 necklace, with $5,000 down and the rest to be paid in installments. Mrs Richards sends this necklace back, accompanied by a note from Mr Richards to Mr Daley, offering to sell him the bonds. The tension causes Mr Richards to fall ill, however, and his wife goes to Daley to make the transaction. While with the Daleys, she breaks down and tells them of the loss and replacement of the necklace; Mrs Daley reveals that the original had only been paste, and the two women rush to tell the good news to Mr Richards.

handed a package by a figure (a servant) who is almost entirely blocked by Richards – only the hand with the box being visible. Even though the second title has cued us that this new action is occurring,

our attention is likely to be split, still partially drawn to the men in the foreground, who seem still to be completing the refusal-to-sell action. They turn as Mrs Daley brings the package forward and Mrs Richards follows. We glimpse the servant exiting at the rear, the only point in the scene at which he is visible. The other three watch as Mrs Daley unwraps the necklace and holds it up toward the camera. This gesture is typical of films of this period, which only occasionally use cut-ins to details like the necklace. In order to guarantee that we will see the object clearly, the actress extends it to the front, in spite of the fact that she is ostensibly displaying it to Mrs Richards, who stands almost behind her, and the two men.

As the shot goes on, Mrs Richards continues to move the necklace about and to smile and exclaim over it; consequently the audience is likely to concentrate on her, even though a series of tiny, quick, but significant gestures occur among the other characters. While Mrs Richards reacts with delight, her husband turns briefly to direct a puzzled glance at Daley (Fig. 15), as if wondering how he can afford such a lavish item. This will be significant later, in motivating the surprise revelation that the necklace is made of imitation diamonds. After this glance, the Richards exchange looks, with the wife hinting in mime that she would like such a necklace, and her husband indicating that it is impossible. Mrs Richards' brief moue of disappointment is fully visible only for a split second, being mostly blocked by Mrs Daley's hand as she continues to flourish the

Fig. 15. *At the Eleventh Hour*

Fig. 16. *At the Eleventh Hour*

necklace (Fig. 16). Again, these glances, however difficult to notice as the scene progresses, are important: they suggest Mrs Richards' covetousness, which will lead her to borrow the necklace, and the couple's inability to afford a genuine diamond necklace. After these actions, the Richards couple departs.

This scene's narration operates quite differently from the linear, long-shot tableau layout of action we have seen at work in *The Inherited Taint*. The filmmakers attempt to bring the action forward toward the 'invisible observer' spectator, both by shooting the locale obliquely into a corner (hence suggesting a deep space that extends forward at either side of the camera) and by beginning the action with sharply distinct foreground and background planes. Yet the staging becomes awkward when the characters line up in the foreground plane, all facing nearly directly toward the front despite the fact that they are supposed to be clustering around to look at an object. Similarly, Mrs Daley's gesture of displaying the necklace to the camera underlines the narration's artifices in providing us with information. Such a staging would be quite common and conventional at this time, and so this scene would not constitute a particularly self-conscious narration. It does, however, hinder communicativeness by making it virtually impossible for us to catch all the action. (I had to watch this brief scene several times on a viewing table to catch the nuances of the acting.)

Subsequent scenes of *At the Eleventh Hour* avoid such dense, competing actions. Most scenes do involve two characters doing separate things in different areas of the locale, but one of them will typically be cued as the more significant.[12] For example, at the reception, the thief stands in a group at the right, surreptitiously glancing at the necklace which Mrs Richards, who stands chatting in another group at the left, is wearing. Here a title, 'The society crook has his eye on the necklace', has cued us to watch him primarily, though a secondary action at the left introduces the hostess of the reception as she admires the necklace. In this case both actions are relatively simple and static.

The subsequent theft scene contains considerable action and a group of people, but its staging carefully motivates the placement of the key gestures in the foreground centre; there is far less confusion here than in the opening scene. A long shot (Fig. 17) shows various guests emerging from the house where the party has taken place; one couple walks diagonally forward along the sidewalk and exits left; a gap behind them allows us to see the Richards couple, with the thief clearly visible behind them. (He is easily distinguishable, being the only person in the scene who is unaccompanied.) As the Richards come forward, instead of exiting left as the first couple had done, they turn and move diagonally front and right, so that they are close enough to the camera for small gestures to be visible (Fig. 18). A space is reserved on the right, into which the

Fig. 17. *At the Eleventh Hour*

Fig. 18. *At the Eleventh Hour*

Fig. 19. *At the Eleventh Hour*

Fig. 20. *At the Eleventh Hour*

thief will move as he pretends to bump into Mrs Richards, removes the necklace, and apologises (Fig. 19). At this point, the Richards turn and walk out of the frame at the left, followed by the thief. Initially, this action seems clumsily staged, since for no apparent reason the couple moves left down the sidewalk, turns right toward the camera, and then goes left again. But in the next shot, we learn the reason for their little zig-zag (Fig. 20): their car is the first of the two parked at the curb. While the first couple seen in the previous shot went straight out left to get to the second car, the Richards moved further forward in order to enter their car. This is a small point, but it does show a desire to motivate the Richards' move forward to the camera realisti-

cally in terms of the scene's overall spatial layout. Hence the fact that the theft takes place in the foreground centre, where we can see it most clearly, seems to arise out of the scene's action. The motivation is only retrospective, since we don't see the car's location until after the cut, but its presence indicates an attempt at creating a narration which is at once communicative and unself-conscious.

Such motivation, however, is not used consistently across the film in all cases where an action needs to be staged in the centre foreground. By comparing three other, similar scenes, we find the mixture of tactics which is typical of the early transitional period. For example, when Mr Richards goes to buy the real diamond necklace to substitute

Fig. 21. *At the Eleventh Hour*

Fig. 22. *At the Eleventh Hour*

Fig. 23. *At the Eleventh Hour*

Fig. 24. *At the Eleventh Hour*

for the original, he stands in front of the counter, which the camera faces straight-on) (Fig. 21). As a result, he must turn away from the salesman to whom he is ostensibly talking in order for us to see his reactions, and no motivation is provided for these movements. It is particularly important that we see his face, because the scene contains a DT, which is cut in at the point when he speaks it: 'I'll pay $5000 down and the rest in installments!' Just before this title, Mr Richards looks out at the camera, puts the necklace down, and begins to move his lips. Given that DTs were still used infrequently in 1912, such clear-cut, visually prominent cues were necessary.[13] This particular shot, however, with its flat back wall and shallow staging, is the most 'oldfashioned' one

in the whole film. Were it not for the low camera height and close framing, the shot would look like a tableau in a film made around 1907. *At the Eleventh Hour*, by the way, like most other films of this period, uses this lower camera height and *plan americain* framing consistently, a tactic which places the characters' heads higher in the frame than would have been usual in the primitive cinema. Thus the framing creates the T-composition, a characteristic of classical filmmaking which was becoming standard quite early in the transition period.[14]

Later scenes in the film use other tactics to keep the action clearly visible. When a messenger delivers the wrapped substitute necklace and Mr Richards' note to Mr Daley, the latter moves from the background to the centre foreground. This action is motivated by the prominent placement of a table; he goes to it and puts the package into a drawer (Fig. 22). His movement also, however, places him close to the camera and facing us as he then reads the note (which we see in an insert); we are thus able to see clearly his delighted expression upon learning that Richards is willing to sell the bonds. The placement of a piece of furniture in the foreground of the scene was probably the most common method the early transitional cinema had for motivating the movements of characters forward to make important actions more visible. It was also common, however, simply to have characters step forward with no motivation, as in the scene when Mrs Richards, by her husband's sickbed, receives Mr Daley's reply. She is tending to Mr Richards, and hence is positioned by his pillow as the maid comes in and hands her the note (Fig. 23). Mrs Richards then steps slightly closer to the camera as she opens and reads it (Fig. 24). We are thus able to see her facial expressions a little more clearly, which is especially important, given that she speaks a line – '*I must* go, I *must!*' – which is not given as an intertitle. To catch this, we have to be able to read her lips.

This variety of methods for staging action in the foreground and turning actors toward the camera demonstrates the transitional cinema's search for the means of achieving a greater degree of communicativeness. *At the Eleventh Hour* is completely typical of films of its period, in that it tries to convey a great deal of information, but sometimes seems to draw upon a narrow range of possible choices of how to do so. A variety of devices is in use, but the film still does not opt for the one major set of techniques which will become crucial as the basis of classical narration – editing within the scene. Aside from intertitles and inserted notes, the only scenes in the film which contain more than one shot use contiguous cuts to show people moving through space: the Richards going to their car after the theft, and the visits of Mr Richards to the jewellery store and the thief to a pawn shop, both of which show the men outside the shops, then inside. Analytical editing and eyeline matches, however, are avoided altogether. Such principles of continuity editing were not unknown at this period, however.

There are also some unexpected narrational tactics in *At the Eleventh Hour*. The National Film Archive print, though not itself coloured, has what I take to be the original tinting and toning notations on little strips of leader between shots at points where the changes would have come. These reveal that colour changes were used to differentiate locales, and that this function was at least as important as the conventional colouring used to indicate night versus day, interiors versus exteriors, and so on. The interiors of the Daleys' house are nearly always black and white, while similar interiors of the Richards' house are toned sepia. Given that a number of scenes involve quick shifts back and forth between these two locales, the changes in toning would help the spectator to keep the action straight. The only exceptions are interiors that take place late at night: one scene at the Richards' is tinted amber, the conventional colour for representing lamp light (after the party, as they decide they must replace the necklace); the second is a scene at the Daleys' (Mrs Richards' 11 p.m. visit to sell the bonds). Night exteriors are mostly tinted blue, though there is one inconsistency: the scene of the thief trying to pawn the stolen necklace presumably takes place late at night, since it is a cutaway from the scene at 11 p.m. where Mrs Richards discovers the truth about the necklace; yet the scene is tinted 'straw', both for the exterior and interior shots. (The reason for this departure from the usual blue for a night exterior is not clear, but it may simply be a mistake, with the person doing the tinting assuming it was a daytime scene. It is even possible that this scene was originally intended as an epilogue to the whole film, then moved to its current position.) Finally, the party locale is tinted amber, again, conventionally appropriate to an evening interior. Tinting and toning provided another narrational level of information which primarily reinforced the spectator's understanding of space, time, and narrative segmentation. Such redundancy would seem to be a trait of the classical Hollywood cinema, but it would be worth a specific study to determine what, if any, were the different functions of tinting and toning between the primitive and classical periods.

The film's narration seems quite knowledgeable and communicative. Certainly it gives us access to more information than any of the characters has. We can move back and forth between the Daley and Richards households, and the narration is able to point the thief out to us before the actual theft occurs; similarly, the cutaway to the thief's discovery in the pawn shop that he has stolen a worthless necklace demonstrates the film's ability to show us disparate events. (This scene also functions to confirm that the necklace is paste and to cover the temporal gap as Mrs Richards and Mrs Daley travel to the Richards' house.) Yet the narration seems not to have privileged information about the nature of the necklace. An expository title in the opening scene states unequivocally, 'Mrs Daley shows her new diamond necklace', even though we later learn that it is not really made of diamonds; this false impression is reinforced when Mr Richards visits the jewellery story and a title calls what he buys 'the duplicate necklace', though again, it is not really a duplicate. This gap in narrational knowledgeability is necessary to the surprise ending. Yet because we learn about the real nature of the necklace so late in the film, we are not likely to recall these earlier instances of an 'unreliable' narration. The narration seems to be wholly knowledgeable.

Fig. 25. *The Tiger*

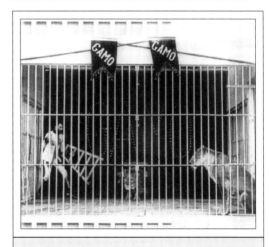

Fig. 26. *The Tiger*

> *The Tiger* (released 11 September 1913)
> Director: Fred Thomson
> Scenario: Marguerite Bertsch
> Supervisor: Ralph Ince
> Cast: Charles Kent (Bardon), Paul Bourgeois (Gamo, an animal trainer), Anita Stewart (Gladys, Bardon's daughter)
>
> ℘ ℘ ℘
>
> While attending a circus performance, Bardon recognises Gamo, an animal trainer who years before had eloped with Bardon's daughter Gladys; after a hard life with the drunken Gamo, she had died. Outside the auditorium, Bardon recalls these events, while on stage Gamo is clawed by a savage tiger. When the circus determines to sell the tiger, Bardon, who has been driven mad by his desire for revenge, buys it and asks Gamo to dine with him and tell him more about the beast. After dinner, Bardon reveals his identity and releases the tiger, which kills Gamo. Bardon himself then dies.

The Tiger

The first half of *The Tiger* consists of a single lengthy scene, in the course of which a great deal of complex exposition is laid out in a leisurely fashion. Unlike *At the Eleventh Hour*, where the initial narrative information is concentrated in a single set-up with several actors' gestures vying for our attention, *The Tiger* strings one bit of information after another. Usually each shot yields only one or two major narrative points. Here we are much closer to the mature classical Hollywood cinema's system of decoupage.

After an introductory medium shot of the tiger, seen outside the story situation, an ET introduces the opening scene: 'At the Hippodrome. By the aid of a photograph which he has carried for years, Bardon recognises in the animal trainer the man who

Fig. 27. *The Tiger*

Fig. 28. *The Tiger*

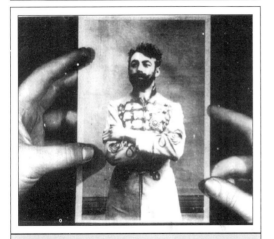

Fig. 29. *The Tiger*

Fig. 30. *The Tiger*

ruined his daughter's life.' This sort of highly compressed summary title would be quite typical of this period, and we might expect to see this action carried out in the shot that follows. Instead, we see Bardon in the audience, staring intently and reacting to something offscreen, behind and slightly to the left of the camera (Fig. 25). This might constitute the 'recognition' portion of the introductory title, but there has been no photograph visible in the shot. (The object under Bardon's left hand on the railing is his program.) An eyeline match to a new shot reveals the cage where Gamo is performing with two lions (Fig. 26). Now we have been given the 'animal trainer' part of the title, with an additional bit of information, the trainer's name, Gamo; he is

redundantly identified by two overhead banners and his name spelled out in lights on the cage's rear wall. By now we might suspect that the opening ET summarises the action in a series of shots, and this is indeed the case. In the scene's third shot, Bardon is seen from a greater distance as he looks at his program, presumably to determine the trainer's name (Fig. 27), then through his binoculars toward the stage. This is followed by another eyeline match to the stage where we see more of Gamo's act from the same framing as Figure 26. (These shots of the cage seem at first to be point-of-view shots, but there is no binocular mask used in this second one, and later framings of the cage are not consistent with Bardon's positions in the auditorium.) Now we re-

Fig. 31. *The Tiger*

Fig. 32. *The Tiger*

Fig. 33. *The Tiger*

Fig. 34. *The Tiger*

turn to Bardon, but in a much closer framing; he lowers the binoculars and takes out a photograph (Fig. 28). An insert from his point of view reveals that the photograph is of Gamo (Fig. 29). The next shot returns us to the same MCU framing of Bardon as he makes an angry gesture at the photograph, puts it away, and looks toward the cage.

At this point, seven shots into the scene, we have reached the end of the recognition portion of the summary given in the initial ET (though the information given there has by no means been exhaustively explored, and the scene will return to it). Now the narration shifts to set up audience suspense over whether or not Bardon will take revenge and (since we suspect he will) speculation over how he will do

so. As shots of Bardon and of Gamo's act alternate, the former's fiendishly gleeful expression (Fig. 30) hints that he may already be plotting his next move. Another shot of the stage from a closer set-up (Fig. 31) shows Gamo prodding a roaring lion through the bars, and we may begin to focus in on a possible method of revenge – one very similar to what Bardon will ultimately utilise.

In the next shot, Bardon gets up, goes up the steps, and out right along the aisle at the top (Fig. 32; the similar long-shot framing of Figure 27 had presumably been introduced in anticipation of this move). He moves jerkily and holds his arm stiffly out, as if he is too wrought up to walk steadily (hinting at his later madness and death). Another shot of

Fig. 35. *The Tiger*

Fig. 36. *The Tiger*

Gamo prodding the lion follows, then a shot of a pair of exit doors. Bardon enters from the left, still looking front and left; he goes through the lefthand door, but immediately his face appears in the little window of the right-hand one, as if he cannot tear himself away from the sight of his enemy (Figs 33–34). Another eyeline match shifts us back to the same view of Gamo against the bars as in Figure 31. An unusual cut takes us back to Bardon, still peering through the window, but seen from the opposite side of the doors. He turns front and emotes (Figs 35–36) and a title, 'Memories' leads us into a major section of the scene devoted to three flashbacks. These, in effect, return us to the last portion of the information summarised in the initial ET, '... the man who ruined his daughter's life'. We see the same view of Bardon, staring upward abstractedly, then lowering his head as a relatively slow fade takes us into the first flashback. It begins with another ET: 'Bardon's daughter elopes with Gamo, an animal trainer.' The last phrase is unnecessary, in that we already know that Gamo is an animal trainer. Yet the sentence as a whole, with its use of the present tense, betrays a considerable assurance that the audience will understand this as the beginning of a flashback; it could have been phrased far more explicitly; for example, 'Years ago, Bardon's daughter had eloped ...'. Three single-shot flashbacks, linked by fades, follow, showing the stages of the affair: the first shows Gladys sneaking out of her house to meet Gamo, the second, the pair in a cheap room with Gamo staggering out drunkenly

Fig. 37. *The Tiger*

and Gladys crying, and the third, Gladys' death, with her father by her bedside. (There have been no additional intertitles.) As Bardon bends over her body, he holds a framed picture prominently out behind his back toward the camera (Fig. 37), then gestures and speaks angrily, finally looking upward; the suggestion is that he is swearing revenge. We also learn in this scene where he got the photograph he used to identify Gamo.

These flashbacks have the effect of demonstrating why Bardon is so upset, motivating the violent revenge he will soon take. They end with a return to the same view of Bardon, who once more gestures wildly at the photograph, then leaves. We have now finally come to the end of the action summarised in the opening ET, but the sequence does not end here. It now returns to the auditorium for an extended series of eyeline matches, alternating views of a group of audience members with views of the stage as Gamo continues his act. A title, 'Prince refuses to work', introduces this, and we see the breakdown of the act, as the tiger claws Gamo and the audience reacts in horror. Another title, 'Gamo has lost his nerve', also covers a whole series of shots, as we see him attempt to re-enter the cage and resume the act, then refuse to continue. Finally, the ringmaster tells the crowd (in a DT placed where it is spoken), 'As Gamo is badly injured and has lost control over the animal, we trust you will pardon the omission of this act'. A final shot of him bowing and exiting rounds off the scene.

This opening scene is remarkable for a number of reasons. It is more extended than most single sequences of films (especially one-reelers) of this period, taking up just over half the film's total length and containing 55 of the surviving print's 91 shots (including intertitles but not credits). This single scene develops in apparently continuous time, occupying the duration of Gamo's act. (The main temporal gap comes at the point where the tiger is brought on in place of the lions, but this seems to be covered by the time of Bardon's recollections.)

One reason for this skillful development of the scene may have to do with a shift in narrational strategies which is apparent here. Rather than summarising a scene's action in detail in advance and then leaving the subsequent images to convey that action briefly (as in the two earlier films), *The Tiger* is more selective about what it tells in advance. This is not only a matter of letting the images, rather than the titles, tell the story. It also means that the spectator will receive bits of information carefully parcelled out over the course of the scene. Indeed, there seems to be a slight conflict in strategies between the ways in which the titles and the decoupage are used. At times the titles still seem to summarise a great deal in advance, as when we learn that Bardon is going to recognise Gamo and then watch the relatively lengthy process of the recognition spread out over several shots. It is easy to imagine that a classical film might handle this scene very similarly in terms of cutting, but would deploy its intertitles differently; for example, the title, 'At the Hippodrome'; the shots of Bardon looking at the stage and

Fig. 38. *The Tiger*

the photo, with shots of Gamo; and another title, 'Bardon recognises the man who years ago ruined his daughter's life'.

The opening ET's final phrase, 'ruined his daughter's life' is, however, evidence of the narration's desire to withhold some information from us, and to present that information gradually in the course of the scene. The phrase suggests that Bardon has reason for revenge, but the scene does not specify that his daughter is dead until the final flashback. Similarly, 'Memories' only introduces the flashbacks themselves, and only the first one has its own expository title, which serves to introduce the new character, Gladys. Thus, although *The Tiger* sticks partially to the early 1910s conventions of the summary intertitle, it also shows an impulse to explore the possibilities of more linear narration. Moreover, the revenge motif, which becomes an important element of suspense quite early on, is never mentioned explicitly in any of the film's intertitles.

This use of introductory titles which do not reveal all the major actions of the upcoming scene intensifies at the transition to the film's second half. After the ringmaster brings Gamo's act to a close, the ET, 'Opportunity is a clever devil' appears. The narration provides information about what this 'opportunity' is within the action of the scene itself: we see Bardon seated in his house reading a newspaper (Fig. 38), followed by an insert of a headline, 'Rajah, the Famous tiger who recently attacked his trainer, has become unmanageable. The beast is

Fig. 39. *The Tiger*

Fig. 40. *The Tiger*

that another character will enter at the left, or that Bardon will simply rise and pace, or that he will exit, and we learn which only at the end of the shot. A classical film would be more likely to handle this situation with balanced framings and then use either reframings or analytical editing or both when Bardon exits – hence creating a less self-conscious narration.

Both this brief scene and the next one, in which Bardon buys Prince (or Rajah?) and invites Gamo to dinner are handled in a much more conventional fashion than was the extended first scene. Each consists of a single framing with inserts or DTs interrupting the action. In the new scene, an ET summarises the action for us: 'Bardon buys the tiger, presumably for a friend's menagerie.' The framing and staging is fairly static until the scene's end, when the tiger cage is carried out. After the initial negotiations between Bardon and the circus owner, Gamo enters, and the scene centres on his description to Bardon of how Prince clawed him; he mimes this by running his fingers, claw-like, down his own chest (Fig. 39). The staging favours Gamo, who faces three-quarters front, while Bardon is seen only in profile. The main purpose of the scene, aside from the purchase of the tiger and the extension of the dinner invitation, is to bring Bardon up to date on the tiger's attack on and hatred of Gamo. (The tiger jumps at Gamo when he enters, and Gamo pokes it with his cane and describes his troubles with Prince at some length.) Bardon had left the theatre before Prince assaulted Gamo, and for a while the omniscient narration had allowed us to know more than Bardon; now he is given all the knowledge that we have.

Indeed, these two short scenes in the middle of the film serve primarily as an expository transition into the second and final extended action, the dinner sequence. In classical fashion, the transition is set up as an appointment, via a dialogue hook. Bardon says to Gamo (in a DT which appears only as a flash-frame in the National Film Archive print): 'Will you dine with me tomorrow night? I wish to learn more about the animal.' He also takes Gamo's bloodied coat, ostensibly as a souvenir, but actually to use in goading the tiger to kill his trainer.

The final scene begins with the ET, 'The hour is at hand', linking to the appointment made in the previous scene. This conforms to the pattern of

for sale.' (An earlier title had called the tiger Prince.) The scene returns to the same framing on Bardon, who gestures excitedly, stands, and goes out. The narration, by the way, has anticipated this exit by placing Bardon initially in the lower right corner of the frame. The narration here is omniscient – from the beginning of the scene it anticipates the character's final exit – and it is communicative – it suggests to us, through the unbalanced framing, that Bardon will act on the news he receives from the paper by going out to buy the tiger. Such a framing also, however, makes for a slightly self-conscious narration, since in order for us to grasp such information, we must notice the imbalance and actively hypothesise about its purposes. After all, it could imply

Fig. 41. *The Tiger*

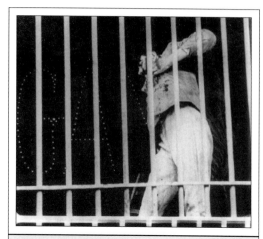

Fig. 42. *The Tiger*

Fig. 43. *The Tiger*

Fig. 44. *The Tiger*

classical scene construction discussed by Bordwell as the 'dangling cause', where one line of action will be set up near the end of one scene and then left open, to be taken up in the next scene.[15] Here the dangling cause permits the narration to glide unself-consciously from one scene to the next. We anticipate what will happen at this dinner (an attack on Gamo using the tiger), and hence the film does not need to use an elaborate summary intertitle. The concentration here is all on suspense rather than on revealing what will happen.

Gamo arrives, and a balanced two-shot turns both men slightly out toward the camera, achieving a modified frontality typical of classical staging (Fig. 40). Like the frontal staging evident in the first

scene of *At the Eleventh Hour*, this technique serves solely to give the spectator a better view of the action, but it is a less noticeable way of doing so. The two men then move to the dining room, a shift signalled by a title, 'In the room without windows, especially built for his purpose'. Dinner is already over, and Bardon reveals his identity. No intertitles accompany this revelation; instead, a second flash-back to the scene of the daughter's death, along with Gamo's terrified reaction, suggest the nature of the conversation. Unfortunately, a bit of footage is missing at this point. Bardon has moved into the next room, where the tiger's cage is concealed. An omniscient narration cuts between the two spaces to show us all the preparations for the attack, with

Bardon goading the tiger and Gamo fruitlessly trying to escape. After the fatal attack on Gamo, the narration becomes quite self-conscious again for Bardon's death: 'Called before a higher judge to render an account of his deeds.' Such self-consciousness is characteristic of the beginnings and endings of classical films.[16]

Beyond conveying narrative information, *The Tiger's* narration contains some devices designed to heighten the impact of certain scenes. For example, as Gamo drags himself to his feet after being clawed by Prince, the camera is placed close to him and tilts up with his movement, ending in a striking low angle (Figs 41 and 42). More elaborately, the scene of the tiger's final attack is dramatically handled, with the tiger suddenly becoming visible in silhouette as the panel in the fireplace is raised (Fig. 43). This effect involved careful planning, as this particular shot is done with undiffused overhead sunlight to achieve the silhouette effect. Other shots in this set are lit differently, with a combination of diffused fill light and directional highlights (as in Fig. 44). Such stylistic flourishes make the film's narration slightly more self-conscious.

Overall, *The Tiger* develops a few devices of classical decoupage to a remarkable extent, though it ignores others altogether. While employing no shot/reverse shot, the film uses eyeline matches extensively in the first scene and intercutting in the final one. Its manipulation of plot order is also quite sophisticated, as when we see the flashbacks in the first scene, then get a repetition of the daughter's death scene later on, or when we first see the tiger's attack on Gamo directly, then watch him re-enact it for Bardon. In contrast to this, the acting is quite extreme – particularly that of Charles Kent as Bardon – as if the actors are still gauging their gestures for a long-shot framing, even though the camera is relatively close to them. The intertitles, moreover, seem somewhat old-fashioned, trying to summarise the action, but being outrun by the lengthy barrages of shots that follow. Those shots are, however, remarkably flexible in their framings, as when we see three different views of Bardon at the beginning, interspersed with his eyeline matches to the act on stage. *The Tiger* thus conforms to what we might expect to find in a film from the middle of the transitional period – an extensive use of a number of options which are becoming more prominent with the development of the classical system, mixed with other devices more typical of the early transitional period.

Conclusions

Let us return to Gaudreault's statement that in the primitive period, 'The narrator was not *conscious* of being a narrator'. By approximately 1917, the narration had, in effect, become fully conscious of being narration; that is, the attempt to present narrative information to the spectator in a clear and linear way was pervasive and systematic in classical films. Yet that impulse to narrate, to inform, was not made obvious to the viewer. As narration became systematic, it found ways of motivating the telling process so that it seemed for the most part to come from within the action of the scene. Only at intervals, which, as we have seen, tend to come at the beginnings and endings of scenes and films, does narration reveal itself self-consciously.

Part of the increasing motivation of a 'reticent' narration came into being through the placement of the spectator within the narrative space. In the primitive cinema, there might be occasions when the action came forward, but the conception was mainly one of simple depth – foreground and background levels of varying distances from the fixed spectator. We have seen how both *The Inherited Taint* and *At the Eleventh Hour* adhere to this conception by avoiding cut-ins; action which needs to be seen in a closer view simply is staged to come forward, sometimes motivated by the placement of a piece of furniture in the foreground. *The Tiger*, however, displays a very different conception of space. The opening scene, with its extended series of eyeline matches, in effect places us almost directly between the two main spaces – the spectators' gallery and the stage – using editing to turn us toward first one and then the other. Moreover, each space is handled with two or more different camera set-ups, so that our vantage on the same characters varies according to the types of action we need to see. The change in our vantage point on the action can also be seen in the modified frontality of *The Tiger's* staging, in comparison with the more directly frontal positioning of action in the two earlier films.

The three films also display the move away from

a heavy dependence on summary expository inter-titles before each shot. Later films allow the summary to cover a whole series of shots and, as in *The Tiger*, to preview the action very selectively. The three films' total number of shots (including written material) versus inserts and intertitles (not counting credits and with brackets to indicate totals taking into account probable missing titles) are summarised in the following table:

	No. shots	No. inserts	No. ETs	No. DTs	Total titles
Inherited Taint	35	2	16	0	16
At the Eleventh Hour	45	5	8	4[5]	12[13]
The Tiger	91	2	11	3	14[?]

The Inherited Taint's proportion of written material (sixteen expository titles and two inserts out of 35 total shots) is fairly high for 1911; by that time, quite a few films were using several shots between titles. *At the Eleventh Hour* and *The Tiger* have similar numbers of titles, both dialogue and expository, but the latter film distributes them across twice as many total shots. The growing use of shot/reverse shot from 1914 on would help to motivate the use of more dialogue titles, which would then take over some of the functions of expository titles.

Classical technique was never really invisible – it was there for anyone to see who wanted to – but it was designed to be unnoticeable. Hence the often repeated notion, put forth by practitioners of film music, film design, cinematography, and so on, that the best film techniques are those which serve their purpose, but which the spectator, upon leaving the theatre, will not remember having heard or seen. This is not a matter of giving the spectator the illusion of being on the edge of a real world, as some recent historians and critics have claimed. Rather, it is a matter of giving the spectator the illusion of witnessing a set of fictional events pure and simple, without the mediation of a narrational system (though that system is, of course, constantly guiding our perception and can call attention to itself in certain situations). Once filmmakers began to formulate this goal as the main criterion for their narration, the transition from primitive to classical filmmaking was under way.▢

Acknowledgment

My thanks to the staff of the National Film Archive, and especially Elaine Burrows, for their help in the research for this essay. It was first published in Italian in *Vitagraph Co. of America: Il cinema prima di Hollywood*, ed. Paolo Cherchi Usai (Pordenone: Edizioni Studio Tesa, 1987).

Notes.

1. David Bordwell, Janet Staiger, and Kristin Thompson, *The Classical Hollywood Cinema: Film Style and Mode of Production to 1960* (London: Routledge & Kegan Paul, 1985), Ch. 14, 157–163.

2. I am not using the term 'narrator' here, since it implies a person doing the telling. Some films do represent a person – either a character or a non-diegetic commentator – as presenting the narrative to us; in such cases, the term narrator would be useful. None of the three films analysed here has such a narrator, however.

3. Bordwell, Staiger and Thompson, *The Classical Hollywood Cinema*, 162–3; the Gaudreault quotation is from his 'Temporalité et narrativité: le cinema des premièrs temps (1895–1908)', *Etudes littéraires*, vol. 13, no. 1 (April 1980): 109.

4. See Kevin Brownlow's *The Parade's Gone By* (New York: Alfred A. Knopf, 1968), 16; Barry Salt, *Film Style & Technology: History & Analysis* (London: Starword, 1983), 106–8.

5. David Bordwell, *Narration in the Fiction Film* (Madison: University of Wisconsin Press, 1985), 57–61.

6. *Ibid.*, 160.

7. *Ibid.*

8. See Jon Gartenberg's 'Vitagraph Before Griffith: Forging Ahead in the Nickelodeon Era', *Studies in Visual Communication*, vol. 10, no. 4 (Fall 1984): 7–23, for a detailed analysis of *Foul Play*.

9. Charles Musser presents an excellent summary of the narrational problems of the primitive cinema and solutions found by filmmakers and exhibitors in his 'The Nickelodeon Era Begins: Establishing the Framework for Hollywood's Mode of Representation', *Framework* no. 22, 23 (Autumn 1983): 4–11.

10. The idea that the film's plot is simple does not seem to be just an impression caused by looking back from a modern perspective. One contemporary review noted that the film's main interest lay in its controversial subject rather than its story:

    A story based upon the popular belief that a taste

for liquor can be inherited. It shows the young man as falling once, but saved through sanitarium treatment and finally triumphant over his weakness in the love of a young woman. While the story is simple the interest in it is increased by the suggestions it makes and the questions it raises. Some will dispute the accuracy of its conclusions, while others will be equally certain that its presentation of the conditions which exist in cases like this are accurate and should be considered as a sort of sermon against the use of liquor, especially by one who may be unfortunate enough to have the inherited taste.

From 'Comments on the Films', The Moving Picture World, vol. 8, no. 15 (15 April 1911): 842.

11. This interpretation is based on inference and convention, however, especially the 'one year' idea. We can only assume that one day, week, or month would be too short a test period. Fiancés typically get one year to prove themselves in such stories.

After making these inferences, I checked the plot synopsis supplied to the *Moving Picture World* by the Vitagraph company. It gives several bits of information which are not apparent in the film; for example, names for the rival (Jack Thurston) and the nurse (Kathleen Holt). The synopsis specifies: 'He asks Kathleen to marry him, she tells him that if he can resist drink for a year, she will consent. He fights his year's battle and wins it, claiming Kathleen as his reward.' From 'Stories of the Films', *The Moving Picture World*, vol. 8, no. 14 (8 April 1911): 784.

12. Even though at times – notably in the first scene – such stagings of multiple actions may cause the spectator to miss some parts of the action, the overall effect is one of dense, compressed action. Again, a contemporary review of the film suggests that viewers of the period might also have found the story to be fast-paced:

It has, as an offering, the usual Vitagraph excellencies. It economises our attention by attending to business, tells the story clearly and dramatically, convinces by good acting, for the most part, and shows excellent photographic portraiture. It makes a good offering.

From 'Comments on the Films', *The Moving Picture World*, vol. 13, no. 7 (17 August 1912): 672.

13. *At the Eleventh Hour* contains three other dialogue titles, two of which come before the shots in which they are spoken, forming summaries of the action to come: 'No trace of it anywhere!' for the scene in which Mr Richards returns to the party to search for the necklace, and 'We'll have to spend our last

dollar to replace it!', introducing the scene in which Mr and Mrs Richards discuss their dilemma. In the jewellery-store scene, the DT could not come at the beginning of the shot, since an ET, 'The duplicate necklace is valued at $12,000', occupies that position. The scene has to make two distinct points here: that the necklace costs $12,000 and that Richards will pay only $5,000 in cash (thus setting up his offer to sell the bonds). The placement of the dialogue title within the scene permits these two points to be made. Later, Mrs Daley's line, 'Why, *my* necklace was only *paste!*' is also cut into the scene at the point when she speaks it, and again lip movement signals the fact that she is talking. Here, too, an ET introduced the scene (At the eleventh hour), but in addition, the line is spoken quite late in a very lengthy shot, and Mrs Daley is not even present when it begins. Placing the DT earlier would not only be confusing, but it would prematurely give away the surprise ending. (There is also a missing intertitle in the scene where Mrs Richards borrows the necklace; this was probably another DT, as it occurs in the middle of a shot.) As with many films of the early 1910s, *At the Eleventh Hour* varies its placement of DTs, but it does so for specific reasons, rather than randomly.

14. That is, the centre and upper third of the composition are the main areas where important actions and facial expressions tend to be placed. See Bordwell, Staiger, and Thompson, *The Classical Hollywood Cinema*, 50–51.

15. Bordwell, Staiger, and Thompson, *The Classical Hollywood Cinema*, 64–66.

16. The very ending of the National Film Archive print of *The Tiger* is missing; we see a brief shot of Bardon which presumably would have ended in his death. A contemporary plot summary specifies:

When the room is at last opened by Bardon's servants they find Gamo a lifeless corpse upon the floor, having been killed by the tiger, while in the next room Bardon, who has been overcome by his emotions, also lies lifeless. His revenge accomplished, Bardon had nothing more to live for.

('Licensed Film Stories', *The Moving Picture World*, vol. 17, no. 10 (6 September 1913): 1090.

This synopsis also states that after Gladys' death Bardon 'had sworn to be revenged upon the coward that had ruined her life', an action which, as we have seen, is strongly implied but never stated in the film.

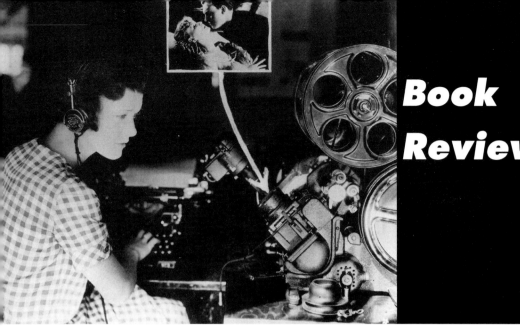

Book Reviews

The Speed of Sound: Hollywood and the Talkie Revolution, 1926–30

Simon & Schuster $30 – by Scott Eyman

John Belton

The Speed of Sound is a departure, of sorts, for author Scott Eyman, whose previous work included biographies of Ernst Lubitsch and Mary Pickford and whose next effort will be a biography of John Ford. The present book deals with Hollywood's transition to sound; it is a history of a technological revolution, not a biography. At the same time, the book is a departure of sorts for trade press publishers, such as Simon & Schuster, who tend to limit their publications on film to biographies.

For the author and the press, however, the departure is more apparent than real. The Speed of Sound is still a biography. It is an account of the 'great men' who innovated sound – of De Forest, Case, Sponable, the Warner brothers, John Otterson (Western Electric executive) and Fox. It is also the story of F.W. Murnau, King Vidor, Rouben Mamoulian, John Gilbert, intertitle writers Katherine Hilliker and H.H. Caldwell, Sam Warner's wife Lina Basquette, actress Esther Ralston and others. It is a history that is driven by heroic individuals. It is not informed by recent work in film historiography; nor does it acknowledge scholarly work on film sound.

Eyman's strategy in writing his history is to establish a cast of characters and to follow their activities from 1926 through 1929 (his history ends in the first few months of 1930). Thus he 'cuts' back and forth from Case to De Forest, from the Warners to Fox as the talkie revolution takes shape. What is unusual in this approach is Eyman's contextualisation of these developments within the slightly larger landscape of the late silent filmmaking of Hollywood. Although it is not initially clear why Eyman spends so much space on silent films in a book on sound, it gradually becomes apparent that these silent masterpieces are meant to exemplify what was lost with the coming of sound.

Thus Eyman deals extensively with Murnau's production of Sunrise (which is a film 'about desire') and Vidor's filming of The Crowd, treating them as examples of the art of the silent cinema. He returns to Murnau to chronicle the making of Four Devils, also silent, and City Girl, to which talking sequences were added. There's very little on Tabu. The inclusion of a section on *Hallelujah* offers Eyman the opportunity to discuss the impact of sound on Vidor's filmmaking, but he doesn't use it. He praises Vidor's use of sound, which 'enabled him to give a voice to the devil he always saw in nature, and in the primary temptation of sex'. But he doesn't pursue the role that sound played in Vidor's evolving vision beyond these enigmatic phrases.

At its best, Eyman's month-by-month portrait of the transition period plunges the reader into the uncertain psychology of Hollywood during this period and reinforces the sense of upheaval experienced by those who worked there. At its worst, it waxes nostalgically over the demise of a medium that had achieved perfection as a means of artistic expression. (Silent films had 'reached a state of liquid perfection, a seamless, impeccable synthesis of style and storytelling'.) He ends the book with a scene in which Doug Fairbanks gazes at a sound-stage covered with 'serpentine wires and cables' and 'menacing microphones' and sighs 'the romance of motion picture making ends here'.

The book is driven by a trade magazine mentality. It's like looking over someone's shoulder as they sit in the library reading *Variety* and *The Film Daily* week by week from 1926–29. The book reports on what was going on then, providing a sort of 'montage of attractions'. The best book on the transition period, Alexander Walker's *The Shattered Silents: How the Talkies Came to Stay*, also relies on this format (and on *Variety*), but since Walker maintains a focus on sound (he doesn't even mention *Sunrise* or *The Crowd*), his history seems more coherent. It is solidly grounded in industrial history and it carefully traces developments in technology, modes of production, and aesthetics in a linear fashion, unlike the shotgun approach of Eyman.

Eyman's explanation of the advent of sound is remarkably simple. It was the result of two major determinants – changes in audiences and changes in technology. With the introduction of radio in 1921 came the development of a new generation of audiences – those with an 'appetite for sound'. For this new generation, sound represented the 'Next Big Thing' in the continually changing face of the movies. By 1926, the major 'bugs' in sound recording and playback technology had been eliminated, making sound films technically viable.

He mentions the efforts of the Warner Bros. and Fox to improve their positions in the industry by innovating sound technology, but he does not build an argument that relies on economics. Eyman is a journalist (he writes for *The Palm Beach Post*). He is not a film scholar or historian; he is clearly not aware of the extensive film scholarship dealing with this period. Consider the question of an economic reading of the forces at work in the transition to sound. He refers several times to Douglas Gomery, who apparently offered him some advice; but the only works by Gomery in his bibliography are *The Hollywood Studio System* and *Shared Pleasures*. He does not cite Gomery's work on sound, ranging from his dissertation to a half-dozen articles published in scholarly journals, which directly addresses the economics of the transition period. He acknowledges two members of the *Film History* editorial board, including Paolo Cherci Usai and Kevin Brownlow. And he has done original research, using the AT&T Archives, the Case Museum, the DeMille Archives, and materials in various film libraries. He also interviewed actors, directors, cameramen, sound engineers, and other relevant industry personnel. But he ignores seminal histories of sound technology by Earl Sponable (in the *SMPTE Journal*), John Frayne/G.R. Groves, Evan Cameron, Patrick Ogle, Steve Neale, Barry Salt, Stephen Handzo and others. It goes without question that he has no unawareness of work by Altman, Bordwell, Chion, Doane, Gorbman, Weis, and Williams, but it is surprising that he doesn't deal with contemporary 'theoretical' responses to the advent of sound by figures such as Arnheim, Balazs, Cavalcanti, Eisenstein, and Pudovkin.

What is valuable about Eyman's book is his incorporation of new data about newly restored Vitaphone shorts and features and his attempts to sort out who did what and when. Robert Gitt of the UCLA Film Archives has given Eyman important information on early Vitaphone technology, techniques developed for recording and playback on discs, and data on sound mixing with the disc system. The Vitaphone restorations change certain features of traditional sound history. The first words spoken in a Vitaphone feature were not Al Jolson's 'Wait a minute, wait a minute, you ain't heard nothing yet!' in *The Jazz Singer* (October, 1927). In *The Better Ole* (October, 1926), the word 'coffee' can be heard (dubbed in to synchronise with an actor's lip movements) and in *The First Auto* (June, 1927), one character addresses another by name, calling him 'Bob'. For some peculiar reason, these important 'firsts' are not in Eyman's text but are buried in a footnote.

Eyman suggests the Mamoulian's 'firsts' – 'the use of multiple microphones' – were not really firsts; 'Warners had been using them for two years'. But it's not clear to me that Eyman understands what Mamoulian did; in *Applause*, Mamoulian recorded dialogue on two *channels*; that's not the same as using two microphones. Eyman tries to pin down the first uses of microphone booms *Hearts in Dixie*, February 1929) and camera blimps (*Painted Heels*, *Dynamite*, 1928). References to such innovations are indicated in the index at the end of the book.

There are no footnotes, so it is not easy to identify his sources for certain pieces of information.

It's hard to tell for whom *The Speed of Sound* is written. It's clearly not addressed to an academic audience; it's too anecdotal and character-driven; it doesn't want to explain the transition to sound; it prefers instead to tell human interest stories about it (will Gary Cooper snub Esther Ralston or not? He doesn't, bless him). But it's too technical for a trade press book. I doubt that general readers would be interested in sound mixing techniques at Warner Bros. in the late 1920s or in the difference between variable area and variable density sound tracks. But perhaps I underestimate the marketplace. I should welcome a trade press book on the coming of sound, but Eyman's book has brought out the cranky academic in me.▢

Technologies of Moving Images

Stockholm, 6–9 December 1998

Call for papers

Proposals are invited on the representation, reception, deployment and dissemination of cinematographic technologies from pre-cinema to digital culture. The conference is organised by the Institute of Futures Studies and Department of Cinema Studies, Stockholm University. The emphasis will be on the inter-relationships between technologies, style and reception: continuities and/or ruptures: the representational interface between technologies – telegraph, telephone, television, video, computer and self-reflexive films; technologies and gender; andtechnologies and bodies. Other key words are: attractions, narrative vehicles, documentaries, and monitoring devices.

Keynote addresses will be given by Lisa Cartwright, Don Crafton, Emily Godbey, Tom Gunning, Mikhail Iampolski, Trond Lundemo, Peter Lunenfeld, Stephen Mamber, Lev Manovich, Michael Renov, Lynn Spigel, Roman Timenchik, Yuri Tsivian and William Uricchio. Their texts will be published by University of California Press, in an anthology edited by Jan Olsson. Conference proceedings will be published, edited by John Fullerton and Astrid Söderbergh Widding.

Those wishing to put forward a paper should submit a 200-word abstract (for a 20-minute presentation) to the conference co-ordinator, Elaine King, Department of Cinema Studies, Box 27062, 102 51 Stockholm, Sweden: fax +46 8 665 0723; e-mail elaine.king@mail.film.su.se no later than 6 April 1998. The abstract should state the title of the proposed paper and indicate what media (film, slide, video, CD-ROM, etc.) will be used in the presentation.

Please contact the conference co-ordinator if you would like to be included on the mailing list.

The Animated Film Collector's Guide

Worldwide sources for cartoons on videotape and laserdisc.

By David Kilmer

In the video age, nearly every film ever made is available on video somewhere. The only problem is finding it. This very helpful book will solve that problem.

This book lists, both by title and producer, sources for many hard-to-find films on video and on laserdisc, both new and out of print. If a title is out of print, this is the only souce or information you will need to track it down.

The Animated Film Collector's Guide also consists of a listing of nearly 3000 animated films and the sources of their video copies. An added bonus is a listing of more than 200 films that have won major prizes at animation festivals and/or placed on animation polls.

David Kilmer has been a lifelong fan and student of animation. He is currently at work on a live action screenplay that incorporates animation.

Available from:

John Libbey & Company Pty Ltd
Level 10, 15–17 Young Street
Sydney NSW 2000 Australia.
Ph: +61 (0)2 9251 4099
Fax: +61 (0)2 9251 4428
E-mail: jlsydney@mpx.com.au

ISBN 1 86462 0021

200 pp.,   S/C,   AUD$45.00,

plus postage:

Within Australia AUD$5.00
Overseas:Airmail AUD$15.00
              Surface AUD$12.00

UPCOMING ISSUES/ CALL FOR PAPERS

Film History 10, 1
Cinema Pioneers
edited by Stephen Bottomore
(deadline for submissions
1 September 1997)

Film History 10, 2
Film and Television
edited by Richard Koszarski
(deadline for submissions
1 December 1997)

Film History 10, 3
Red Scare
edited by Daniel J. Leab
(deadline for submissions
1 March 1998)

Film History 10, 4
Special issue on the Centennial of Cinema Literature

Film History 11, 1
Film Technology
edited by John Belton
(deadline for submissions
1 September 1998)

The editors of *FILM HISTORY* encourage the submission of manuscripts within the overall scope of the journal. These may correspond to the announced themes of future issues above, but may equally be on any topic relevant to film history.

FILM HISTORY

Back issue and subscription order form

PLEASE SUPPLY:

.... Subscription(s) to *Film History*
      at Institutional/Private rate (please specify)
      Surface/Airmail (please specify)
.... Back issues of the following volumes/issues
....
....
I enclose payment of AUD$/US$ ....
Please send me a Pro-forma invoice for:
AUD$/US$ ....
Please debit my Access/Master Card/Visa/
American Express/Diner's Club credit card:
Account no..Expiry.........
Name ....
Address ....
....
....
.... Zip/Postcode ....

Signature ....Date ....
(This form may be photocopied)

SUBSCRIPTION RATES & BACK ISSUE PRICES

Institutional Subscription rates:
   All countries (except N. America)
   Surface mail AUD$172
   Airmail AUD$194
   N. America
   Surface mail US$151   Airmail US$172
Private Subscription rates (subscribers warrant that copies are for their PERSONAL use only):
   All countries (except N. America)
   Surface mail AUD$66
   Airmail AUD$88
   N. America
   Surface mail US$59   Airmail US$79
Back issues: All issues available – Volumes 1 to 9:
US$20/AUD$24 each number.

JOHN LIBBEY & COMPANY PTY LTD,
Level 10, 15–17 Young Street
Sydney, NSW 2000, Australia
Telephone: +61 (0)2 9251 4099
Fax: +61 (0)2 9251 4428
E-mail: jlsydney@mpx.com.au

FILM HISTORY

An International Journal

Aims and scope

The subject of *Film History* is the historical development of the motion picture, and the social, technological and economic context in which this has occurred. Its areas of interest range from the technical and entrepreneurial innovations of early and pre-cinema experiments, through all aspects of the production, distribution, exhibition and reception of commercial and non-commercial motion pictures.
In addition to original research in these areas, the journal will survey the paper and film holdings of archives and libraries worldwide, publish selected examples of primary documentation (such as early film scenarios) and report on current publications, exhibitions, conferences and research in progress. Many future issues will be devoted to comprehensive studies of single themes.

Instructions to authors

Manuscripts will be accepted with the understanding that their content is unpublished and is not being submitted for publication elsewhere. If any part of the paper has been previously published, or is to be published elsewhere, the author must include this information at the time of submittal. Manuscripts should be sent to the Editor-in-Chief:

   Richard Koszarski
   Box Ten
   Teaneck, NJ 07666, USA
   E-mail: filmhist@aol.com
except for submissions to thematic issues directed by one of the Associate Editors.

The publishers will do everything possible to ensure prompt publication, therefore it is required that each submitted manuscript be in complete form. Please take the time to check all references, figures, tables and text for errors before submission.
Form: Authors are requested to submit their manuscripts on diskette – IBM format (preferably) or Apple Macintosh – together with an original and two copies of the paper, in English,